Wild-Card Poker

♣　♦　♥　♠　♣　♦　♥　♠　♣　♦

Wild-Card Poker

♣ ♦ ♥ ♠ ♣ ♦ ♥ ♠ ♣ ♦

HUGH ZACHARY

THE STEPHEN GREENE PRESS

BRATTLEBORO, VERMONT

It is published by The Stephen Greene Press, Brattleboro, Vermont 05301.

Library of Congress Cataloging in Publication Data
Zachary, Hugh.
    Wild-card poker.
    Includes index.
    1. Poker. I. Title.
GV1251.Z3   795.4'12   74-27459
ISBN 0-8289-0250-X
ISBN 0-8289-0249-6 pbk.

75 76 77 78 79 9 8 7 6 5 4 3 2 1

♣ ♦ ♥ ♠ ♣ ♦ ♥ ♠ ♣ ♦

Cap'n Larry Stubbs started the game with Cap'n Ray
Lineberry and Rosa, Bob Hatch and other crew
members of the Army's Navy at Southport. This
book is for them, and for: Bill and Ester Dorsett,
Bill and Dot Cupit, Mebin Martin the Gambling
Lady, Ruth Sochacki, Clarence and Glenna Pegram,
Tom Tyler, Buzz Thompson and all the visitors who
came to contribute to the Club. And for Elizabeth,
my wife, who did all right until we started Acey-
Deucy night.

Contents

CHAPTER I

Wild-Card Poker

PEOPLE LIKE TO play poker, to gamble, even if it is for low stakes. To a growing number of social poker players, however, nothing is duller than conventional stud and draw poker played with a limit. Since most friendly games are played with a nickle or a dime limit on any one bet with a maximum of three raises per bet, the game quite often becomes mere showdown, with all players staying for the last card. It's almost impossible to drive out a poor poker player with a bet of a nickle or even with three raises of a nickle each. Thus there is no chance to display skill, to exercise a knowledge of character, or to bluff.

Draw and stud poker are money games. In a game where the chips are rated at the dollar and not the penny level, and a player may bet an unlimited amount, or, perhaps, the amount he has at the table, money can talk. A player who pushes a huge pile of chips to the center of the table and says, "That's my bet," is being very, very eloquent even if he is using one-syllable words. In a money game, if a player bets the farm on a bluff, someone is going to have to risk a lot of

1

loot, enough to hurt, in order to call him a liar. In a nickle-limit game with three raises allowed per bet, any player in the game can call you a liar for a few cents. Anyone with high optimism and a long chance can stay and draw, and this changes the character of the game entirely.

In a money stud game, aces back to back on the first two cards can bet the farm and stand a good chance of winning the ante and a couple of calls before the other players give in to the almost certain high pair. In a low-limit game, everyone stays and there are some fantastically lucky draws, and two aces back to back can very easily become second best to two pairs.

Stud with a limit is impossible. Draw with a limit is on a par with Old Maid or Slapjack.

WILD GAMES AND WILD PLAYERS

Rather than put up with the humdrum of low-limit conventional games, more and more poker players in social situations are looking for added elements of excitement above and beyond traditional poker. Old, familiar games are being spiced up by the addition of one or more wild cards and new games of a more complex nature are being added to the old list of poker games which begins with Bluff Poker and ends with such exciting items as Deuces Wild, or, perhaps, with Baseball.

Adding wild cards to traditional games makes for an element of uncertainty. Creating new games of a more complex nature makes the fall of the cards more suspenseful.

My wife and I have had a wild-card game going for eight years. The cast of characters changes now and then as players move away or find out that they can't compete in a wild-card game. Our stakes are small. Bets are limited to a nickle, except in specific situations usually involving progressive betting games, and only three raises are allowed per bet. In an evening a very poor player can lose ten or twelve dollars, but a good player can limit his losses, on the blackest of nights, to two or three dollars. A winning evening of five dollars is a good one.

In our game money is used mainly to keep score. The amount of money that changes hands is not large enough to become important in itself. We don't have any professional gamblers trying to crash our little club in an effort to augment income, but we do have an old-time card sharp and big money player who passes the deal each time because he can take an ordinary deck and place all four aces at will. He's played in games where real money covered the table top, but now that he's reformed he finds that wild-card poker is a pleasant way to spend an evening. The increased action in wild-card games helps to make him forget that it's only two dollars instead of two hundred or two thousand out there in the pot.

Why do people set aside one or two nights per week to sit around a table and watch cards fall, betting huge amounts up to twenty cents? Since I'm not qualified to undertake a study of the psychology of gambling and gamesmanship, let's just say that it's the fall of the cards. Most of the members of our poker club are bridge players of one degree or another. At least one is an inveterate gambler who will bet a small amount of money on almost anything from bingo to high card on a cut. A mild, pleasant professional man, a pillar of his church, uses poker as an outlet for hidden aggressive feelings, thumping down five aces to top a high-betting five kings with a snarl and flashing eyes. Other members play for purely social reasons, just for the company.

For various reasons, six to eight of us meet at least once a week and watch the fall of the cards, and we have found, as have so many other social players around the country, that wild-card poker is the answer to the limited possibilities offered by traditional forms of the game. We've been known to organize people right out of the club for insisting on dealing stud or draw straight each time the deal came around to them.

I'm not saying that the addition of a few wild cards to a card game can replace the gut-level tension of backing three deuces against a possible straight with several hundred dollars. But I do stoutly maintain that there has to be some interest in a poker game, and if it isn't provided by high stakes, then variety and the possibility of holding an important hand on each deal can make a two dollar pot much more interesting.

I love poker stories. In a movie or a book a good poker hand can be built up into true suspense and can last for long, delicious minutes. I wish I could have seen a game which was described to me recently. It was played in Saigon, and two dream hands bumped heads to the tune of a lot of back pay and some travel money. One player held four queens in seven card stud, two down and two up. Naturally, he bet the farm. Only one man stayed. The opponent, who was a close friend of the holder of four queens, had one king up. His other three up-cards were widely spread. It was evident that a straight flush was impossible. He would have had to have three clubs in the hole to have a flush. To have a full house, since he showed no pair up, he would have had to hold a pair in the hole matching one of his up-cards plus another match for an up-card, a very unlikely possibility. The odds against his holding three of a kind in the hole to match an up-card were astronomical. However, since he was a friend of the holder of the four queens, he said, "Don't bet any more, buddy. I've got you whupped."

Four queens, thinking that his opponent was holding two pairs or a flush or a fluke full house at the best, bet all the money he had plus a few months' future pay.

Naturally, there were three kings in the hole to make a total of four. A lot of money changed hands and a friendship died.

Such a dramatic situation arises just often enough in stud or draw poker to make the game an adventure when real money is at stake, but both those players could play stud poker the rest of their lives without ever again holding four face cards of a kind.

In wild-card poker four kings would, in many cases, be a loser. In some wild-card games a straight flush is a poor risk, a royal flush only so-so, and four of a kind a throw-in. In some games five of a kind is a cinch only when they are aces, and in a game with enough wild cards five aces could be good only for a tie.

"THAT AIN'T POKER!"

Because of the increased possibility for important hands, a lot of average poker players can't handle wild cards. I've seen a man throw down his cards and try to break down a door getting out when, in a dealer's choice game, the dealer called out "One-Eyed Jacks, the Man With the Ax and a Pair of Natural Sevens Takes It All." And that's a tame one as wild games go.

"That ain't poker!"

I've heard those words from many lips. They usually come, accompanied by considerable profanity, from some member of the hairy-chest set who has been holding up the game having all sorts of delirious fun scratching himself and sweating out the fifth card in a hand of draw which he has dealt after losing five dollars on simple wild-card games.

Poker, you see, has always been one of those manly pursuits. To play poker, you have to smoke a cigar, loosen your tie and grow a two-day stubble of beard, get red-eyed, drink whiskey out of the bottle, talk out of the corner of your mouth and curse joylessly while using thirty minutes in contemplation of another fellow's hand to figure out if he's bluffing or if he really does have that four in the hole to complete his straight.

Every now and then I run into a poker player who actually maintains that seven card stud has no place in a man's game of real poker. Anytime I hear such an asinine remark I tab the speaker as either a compulsive gambler who will stay and see all raises when the best he could hit is one low pair, or a man so lacking in card sense that counting past five is too much for him.

"That ain't poker!" they shout.

Oswald Jacoby is the only poker authority I've ever read who recognizes the increased skill and knowledge required for wild-card poker. In a session where the game changes with each dealer the task of knowing what should sink an opponent becomes much more difficult. Most poker books deal almost exclusively with stud and draw. Jacoby does list a few wild-card games, including one very good one called Cincinnati Liz which we call Fifty-Five and spice up by adding jokers and progressive betting. But most so-called authorities turn up their noses at sissy games like Deuces Wild, a game which is so tame a confirmed wild-card player won't ever bother to deal it.

I'm sure that wild-card poker will never take Las Vegas by storm. When big money is being risked, the bet alone is excitement enough, and stud allows the scientific player to lose his homestead playing the odds, gives the bewhiskered, cigar chewing big-time gambler a release for his gambling urge and provides the professional a living. I'll play stud with the boys for table stakes and I won't ring in one wild-card game on them so long as they don't try to limit my knowledge of the game by setting a limit on the betting so that some idiot can afford to draw to an inside straight against my two pairs. Furthermore, I'll invite any of the that-ain't-poker crowd to sit in with us any Tuesday or Friday night and I'll bet any sizable amount on the side that one of our lady members will walk away with some of that great stud player's money. And all the screams of "That ain't poker" won't erase the fact that a mighty gambler has fallen because he can't grasp the difference between the value of a straight in five card stud and in five card stud with the low hole-card wild.

The champion loser in our eight year marathon game was a one-timer, a guest who could afford to and did play in a big game over the county line where thousands of dollars often changed hands. He dropped almost twenty dollars between seven-thirty and eleven in the evening. That was, to him, a trifling amount of money, but he left his pride behind as he departed saying, "That ain't poker."

Well, admittedly, it isn't traditional poker, but it's more entertaining than television and any number up to eight can play. To make wild poker interesting you need a minimum of five players, but six to seven make for the best games. Small-stakes poker can satisfy a lot of needs in human nature, the need for companionship, the compulsion to risk money betting on something, the need to be aggressive in a bloodless way. Whatever the rationale for it, wild-card poker is here to stay, and it's popular with women as well as with men.

WHAT IS A WILD CARD?

A wild card is simply a card or cards which can be used as any other card in the deck. Games are played with as few as one and as many as fourteen wild cards. A wild card may be a joker. It can be any card in the deck. Deuces Wild is one of the older and more familiar forms of wild-card poker. In stud or draw all four deuces are designated wild. Thus, four aces and a deuce become five aces, with the deuce acting as the fifth ace. Ace, king, queen, jack of hearts and deuce of any color become a royal flush.

In some older poker books the rules allow the use of the double-ace flush. Thus, ace, deuce of any color, king, ten, five of hearts would be an ace-ace-king-high flush and would beat an ace-king-high flush. I think the double-ace flush is the mark of amateurism in wild-card poker and it's never allowed in our games. Everyone knows that there are not two aces of hearts in a deck of cards, so it seems logical to me to disallow the double-ace flush.

Jokers

Two extra cards come with every deck. Many games utilize these two cards, the jokers, as wild cards. It's fairly standard to call the joker a joker when it's wild all the way—that is, when it can be used as *any* other card in the deck. When the joker is wild only with aces, straights and flushes, it's usually called the Bug. It's a good idea to have an understanding about jokers in any game. Our house rule is that the joker acts as the Bug, wild only with aces, straights and flushes, unless otherwise stated by the dealer or unless there are one or more other wild cards in the game. If there is a wild card other than the joker, then the joker is also wild all the way and can be used as any card in the deck. With this rule stated as house policy it is not necessary to ask "How about the jokers?" on each deal.

Other Wild Cards

Any card in the deck may be designated wild. However, there is usually some reason for selecting a particular card to be wild. For example, in Dr. Pepper, tens, twos and fours are wild because of the old Dr. Pepper advertising slogan—*re-*

member Dr. Pepper time at ten and two and four. In 7-Up, sevens are, naturally, wild.

Some wild games make use of the standard design of the cards. There are, for example, four jacks in the deck, two of them full-face and two in profile. Thus, when a dealer calls one-eyed jacks wild, there will be two wild cards—the pro- file jacks which show only one eye. The possibilities are limited only by the design of the cards and the imagination of the player.

Wild cards may be picked out of the blue, but such prac- tice is frowned upon. A player could call sixes and eights wild, but there's no little rhyme involved in that call and no connection with anything which would give a certain logic to the selection.

Another game—Deuces and Jacks and the Man With the Ax—makes a rhyme and utilizes card design. Only the king of diamonds carries a battle-ax. So, in that variation, all four deuces, all four jacks and the king of diamonds would be wild.

ODDS? WHO KNOWS?

I have not the faintest idea how to figure the odds against drawing five aces in a game with twelve wild cards. It would be even more difficult to calculate the odds in a game such as Follow the Queen, where the wild card can change during the course of the deal. Therefore, there will be no attempt at making odds tables here. In any wild-card game the odds against holding a particular hand are reduced considerably.

At the end of the section which explains each wild-card game I will make a general statement as to what *should* win the pot in that particular game based on a game with six to eight players. These little statements should not be taken as absolute guides. In wild-card poker the only sure thing is that there will be one or more winners.

Wild-card poker is more of a guessing game than conventional poker. Take one small example: You're playing a very simple game, Five Card Stud with Deuces Wild. You hold two large pairs. Your opponent shows four cards to a straight. He needs a six to have his straight and two sixes have shown in the up-cards of other players. In traditional poker that would cut your opponent's chances of having a six in the hole to two cards out of fifty-two. However, with deuces wild, he has four more chances to have a six in the hole. I would never bet the farm against his not having a deuce. The addition of four wild cards has more than doubled his chances.

CHAPTER II

Some Basic Rules

I A M assuming that anyone who is ready to graduate to wild-card poker is familiar with the basic principles of stud and draw. Most of the games in this book are children, legitimate or otherwise depending on one's point of view, of these traditional forms of the game. Whatever the game, wild-card play is based on poker, and the rules of poker apply. Nevertheless, there are certain rules pertaining to wild-card poker which differ from or augment the laws of traditional poker. Before passing to the wild games themselves, we had best get clear about some of the distinctive features of wild-card play.

RANK OF THE HANDS

In wild-card poker we add an entirely new rank of hands. Even if there's only one wild card in the deck there is the possibility of holding five cards of a kind. Five of a kind always beats a royal flush, the highest hand possible in traditional poker. In wild games, the hand-rank is as follows.

1. Five of a kind: Beats anything except five of a kind of equal rank. Tie hands split the pot or that portion of the pot to which they apply.
2. Royal flush: Ace, king, queen, jack, ten of the same suit.
3. Straight flush: Five cards in the same suit in numerical sequence. For example, five, six, seven, eight, nine of hearts.
4. Four of a kind.
5. Full house: Three of a kind and a pair. The rank of rival full houses is determined by the rank of the three of a kind, or, if the three of a kind holdings are the same, by the pair.
6. Flush: Five cards, not in numerical sequence, in the same suit. Rival flushes are ranked by high cards. For example, ace, jack, and three small cards would beat ace, ten, and three small cards.
7. Straight: Five cards, not in the same suit, but in numerical sequence. Rival straights are ranked by high cards.
8. Three of a kind.
9. Two pairs.
10. One pair.
11. A hand in which nothing is matched. Ranked on high cards.

IN CASE OF TIES

Because of the large number of wild cards in some games, identical hands are not uncommon in wild-card poker. The following rules are important in evaluating tied hands.

Only five cards play poker. The game itself might consist of ten cards, but when show-down time comes, only five cards may be used in making the poker hand. Regardless of the number of cards involved in the game, when two players have identical hands in five cards it is a tie. It is not permissible to use a sixth card as a kicker to break the tie.

In poker, the rank of the suits is the same. A royal flush in clubs is as potent as a royal flush in spades. Some bridge players might want to break a tie between two royal flushes by resorting to bridge-type rankings of the suit. Not in poker. It's a tie.

A hand containing wild cards is as strong as a hand of the same rank containing only natural cards. Back in the dim, dark days of early wild-card poker some genius who didn't really like wild cards said that a natural ace would outrank an ace represented by a wild card. Thus, an ace-high flush with a joker would lose to an ace-high flush with a natural ace and the same lower cards. Not so. Wild cards rank just as high as natural cards which they represent. Ties may not be broken in this manner.

A wild card may be counted as an ace although not matched by a natural ace. This gives the lie to another antique rule made up by some feeble-minded stud player back in the Stone Age. According to this rule an ace-high hand in, say, five card stud, would beat a joker-high hand of the same value in which nothing was paired. Not so. A joker may be an ace even when it's not paired with a natural ace, and it holds its own with any other card.

IRREGULARITIES ON THE DEAL

The laws of poker regarding dealing, exposed cards, etc., are detailed in many books. One good one is *Oswald Jacoby on Poker,* written by one of the top authorities on both poker and bridge. In general, the laws of poker apply to wild-card play. In social games no one is playing for blood, so the rules can be relaxed and easy, but there should be some understanding about what to do in case of exposed cards, etc. Exposing just one card on the deal can be more serious in wild-card poker than in straight games. An exposed wild card reveals a certain amount of power and in a game with a pot splitter, exposure of the splitter can tell which player will win half the pot. So rules are necessary. Sloppy playing and dealing can be very irritating even in friendly situations. No one should get too excited if a player folds out of turn, but it is a good idea to bet in turn and ante in turn just to keep the pot straight. It's not financially disastrous if a player forgets to ante his nickle, but it is irritating to some players. I, for example, have lived with a counting compulsion all my life and I habitually count the ante in any game.

Cards exposed on the deal can be handled by the old poker adage "There's no mistake in poker." Thus, a player keeps his exposed card. If the game is being dealt with some cards down and some up, the exposed card can be replaced with a down-card at the next deal around the table.

In a relaxed game if a player is dealt too few cards the problem can be solved by giving him one or more off the top of the deck. If a player has been given too many cards the situation can be handled as follows:

1. If the player with too many cards has not looked at his hand, the dealer may take a card at random from the hand and either burn it or put it on top of the deck.

2. If the player has looked at his hand and no betting has taken place, he may call a misdeal.

3. If the player neglects calling attention to his surplus

until after the betting is begun, he is not to be allowed to play his hand under any circumstances.

THE SPLITTER

Many wild-card games are played with an automatic pot splitter. One familiar form of splitting the pot between two winners is High-Low, in which the high poker hand and the low poker hand share equally in the spoils.

Often, a particular card in a suit is designated as the splitter. It's dealer's choice, the splitter, as is the game. If the dealer calls the low spade as the splitter, then the deuce of spades is good for half the pot regardless of high hands. If the deuce is not out, then the three of spades would win half the pot.

Any card can be called the splitter, but usually it's the high or low card in a suit, as above. It is permissible to call one particular card as splitter, such as "four of spades *only* splits the pot." Thus the four of spades would have to fall in order for there to be a splitter. This method of splitting is not as successful as calling a high or low splitter, since many players will stay and call bets if, for example, they're holding the king in the splitting suit with the high card splitting.

It may seem to be a contradiction when I state that one purpose of calling a splitter in wild-card games is to build the pot, since one of the prerequisites for playing wild-card poker is low stakes. But calling a splitter does help to build the pot and make for more interest. Playing with a splitter also helps to distribute the wealth. The poorest player can win half the pot if he's sitting on the deuce of spades with the low spade splitting.

THE ANTE

In some circles, peopled mostly by antique players who spend hours playing one hand of five card stud, the dealer is required to ante for all players. Frankly, I think this is silly as all hell. In low-limit poker, in order to build a pot, every player antes for every hand. The ante is dealer's choice and may range up to the stated limit which, in our games, is a nickle.

Some players have an abhorrence for particular games and make a point of not playing them. This is rather poor sportsmanship, since most players play games they like less than others. If you just can't abide a particular game please don't say, "Deal me out" when it is called. Make the ante and then fold your cards quietly.

PLAYING LIGHT

In low-stake games a player plays light for various reasons and not, usually, because he is broke. Perhaps he doesn't have the proper change or he thinks that he has a part of the pot won and doesn't want to have to dig into his pocket for more money. Whatever the reason, playing light is usually allowed in friendly games.

Mechanically, playing light is merely drawing money out of the pot in the amount of the bet in order to keep track of the total of bets which an individual player has called. The light amount is kept separated in front of the player until time for the pot to be collected.

If a player has called thirty cents in bets without having money of his own to put in the pot, he has thirty cents in lights in front of him. He owes the pot double that amount, counting the light amount itself. His obligation is not satisfied merely by pushing his lights back into the pot. Since the light amount indicates how much he owes the pot, and itself came from the pot, he must replace it and then match the light amount with money of his own.

If a player is light and wins half the pot, his obligation can be met by giving his lights to the other winner. For example, he's light fifty cents. He owes the pot the light amount of fifty cents plus fifty cents of his own. If he put a dollar into the pot to satisfy his obligation he would get fifty cents of it back on the split. He gives the other winner his fifty cents in lights and takes nothing himself, and thus his debt of fifty cents to the pot is cancelled. If the light player loses, he pays the total he owes before the split, or he gives fifty cents to each winner.

If there are more than two winners and one of them is playing light, the simplest way of handling the situation is to have the light player make his lights good in the pot before attempting to split. It's astounding how much confusion can be caused by such situations.

Playing light is not the best policy, but most people don't object if it's handled properly and without confusion. At times it can save time and make the game move faster.

A FEW MINOR POINTS

In a continuing game among friends most disputes can be handled by consulting Jacoby or Hoyle, if such disputes pertain to the laws of poker. However, it must be remembered that the laws of politeness, often as much mistreated as the laws of poker, also apply.

Etiquette

I have some pet peeves which might serve to warn others about some of the pitfalls of social poker. First of all, when I meet with our group I'm meeting with one prime object in mind. I came to play poker. The poker table is not the place for gossip, long jokes or the compulsive talker. So, with that as a starting point, here's my list of rules for behavior at the poker table.

1. Please limit the conversation to such brilliant statements as: "I'll see that bet" or "I'll raise five."
2. Pay attention. If you don't understand the game, don't hesitate to ask, but if you'll listen as the dealer explains, you'll catch it most of the time.
3. Keep the game moving. Take time to think it through, but don't submit the players to elaborate "sweating it out" pantomimes on every hand.
4. Don't waste time bleeding over what might have been. The other players are not really interested in what you would have hit if you'd stayed. That's history. Deal the cards.
5. Don't pass your hand all around the table to show those who have dropped out what you have. They'll see soon enough when showdown time comes.
6. If you're using coins instead of chips, as is the custom in most low-stake games, try to call the bet with the exact change. Don't toss in five pennies when you have a nickle available. The more small change there is in the pot the longer it's going to take to split it. In an evening, many minutes can be consumed by two splitters counting pennies.
7. Ladies, keep the refreshments simple. It's hard to deal around a full-course dinner.
8. Bet and ante in turn.
9. Please, no partnership poker. It's poor sportsmanship for a husband to raise on nothing because he knows his wife has the winning hand or the splitter.
10. If you're out and another player does you the courtesy of showing you his hand, please don't comment one way or the other.
11. Don't ask to see a player's hand if you're out unless he offers to show it to you.

12. Go with the group on small matters. If seven of eight players play the games with jokers in the deck, it can be irritating for them if you insist on removing the jokers each time you deal. Moreover, it consumes time which could be used in dealing another hand.

13. Don't tell the other player how stupid he was to call because, after all, it's his money. If he wants to be stupid and call a bet when he's clearly beaten, he's the one who is paying for it and he deserves to be allowed to be stupid without having attention called to it.

14. Losers have a traditional right to cry, but please don't wet the table with your tears. It makes the cards sticky.

15. No drunks, please.

16. If you don't know how to play poker and want to learn, watch from the sidelines until you at least know the difference between a flush and a straight.

17. If you don't like wild cards, stay the hell out of our games. You were warned in advance that we play wild-card poker, not nickle-limit stud and draw.

18. Settle all debts before the game breaks up.

19. On the showdown, call your hand in turn. The last bettor or raiser calls first, then the call goes around the table to the left. Waiting until someone to your left calls his hand because he thinks you're out of the game is incredibly bad sportsmanship and has, in at least one case to my knowledge, resulted in fisticuffs.

20. If you're having trouble figuring your best hand, remember that in friendly games the cards speak for themselves. Lay down your hand and let the other players help you read it.

21. In games where all cards are dealt face down the dealer should collect all folded hands and put them either on the bottom of the deck or on a discard pile

to eliminate confusion about who is in and who is out. There is a great temptation, I know, to hold a folded hand to see what would have developed if you'd stayed in. While this can work out all right, it should be the responsibility of the individual player to keep his cards off the table or to one side so that other players won't think he's still in the game.

Who Buys The Cards?

I hate to play with limp cards. In this discount age the best poker cards can be bought rather cheaply in discount houses. It seems foolish to me to try to make a deck of cards last forever.

One method of assuring a fresh deck for each game is to pinch the first few pots to pay for the deck. By taking a nickle from each pot until the deck is paid for, the early winners pay for the cards and no one really feels it. And there's a nice, stiff, fresh pack of cards for each meeting of the club.

Some clubs with the same members playing on a long term continuing basis pinch the pot for refreshments, especially if one member owns a game room and a poker table where most of the games take place. This can become irritation-plus unless there is a standard menu. I prefer keeping the refreshments confined to the coffee and potato chip level. Other clubs spend much time deciding whose turn it is next meeting. This, too, can become a drag and is best left to the wives in the group.

SUMMING UP

Wild-card poker is mostly a social activity and is usually played for low stakes. However, as in most gambling activity, there is always the temptation, especially among the losers, to raise the stakes. In a social game this temptation should be resisted. Don't go beyond raising the ante to a dime on the last hand or, perhaps, giving the losers one more chance to get even in a hand of showdown for a quarter at the end of the evening.

It is also advisable to set regular hours of play. Set a starting time and a closing time and stick to them. Our meetings start at seven-thirty and end at eleven on week nights and extend to twelve on Friday or Saturday night when none of the members is to be faced by an early-ringing alarm the next morning.

In the following sections of this book I will try to explain in detail all the games which have kept our members interested in wild-card, low-stake poker for eight years. One or two of the games are original. Some are old standards and some are interesting variations on standards. The games have been gathered from diverse sources, but I do not claim that they represent all possible wild-card games, only a representative cross section of wild games, including, it is hoped, the most interesting ones which seem to wear well under the test of continuous play.

It is to be remembered that there are no hard and fast rules for wild-card games. Baseball, for example, has dozens of variations. However, within a club, there should be standard rules for each game. House rules should be established so that one dealer won't say, "Roll your fours for a secret," and another dealer say, "No secrets for fours."

In this book I will detail the games as we play them or, in a few cases, as I think they should be played. The reader may feel free to change minor points. In general, this book is intended as a guide; it does not have the ambition of standardizing all wild-card poker games.

It's been said that a good wild-card poker player is a mixture of verve, nerve and cupidity. This book is intended for that sort of player. If it serves to add just one more exciting game to the repertoire of a fine, dedicated wild-card player I will judge it a success.

A book quite naturally reflects the opinions and prejudices of the author and this one is no exception. While I have listed many wild-card games and several variations of some games, I have come to favor some and to despise others. Each player is free to form his own opinion, but to give a loose guide for those who have not played wild-card poker to a great extent, I will rate the various games for interest and action as I see them.

In rating the games I have considered:

1. The size of the pots built by various games. A two dollar pot is more interesting than a fifty cent pot.

2. Suspense and doubt. It's much easier to figure possibilities in a five card stud game than in a seven card game with fluctuating wild cards.

3. The possibility of holding powerful hands.

4. The ability of a game to hold interest over a long period of play.

A rating of four stars (★★★★) is tops in my system. I include many games which don't rate a single star simply because they do offer variety and because a difference of opinion is what makes betting interesting in the first place. A game which I don't rate one star could be a winner for someone.

I was tempted to start the list of games with the four-star blockbusters and then taper off, but in the end I decided to begin with the simpler games and build through to more complicated games. This lends itself to a certain orderliness, but please feel free to skip over the more mundane items to the big pot builders.

In the sections dealing with the more complicated games I have included a paragraph or two under the heading

METHODS OF PLAY. The experienced card player will find this section superfluous. However, each complicated wild-card game comes complete with its own peculiarities and, while I make no claims toward being the ultimate authority on wild-card poker, these little commentaries are based on my experience over a period of years. My methods seem to work most of the time. I've kept accurate records of my poker money over a period of years, and I'm well ahead of the game.

CHAPTER III

Wild Games
Based on Five Card Stud

FIVE IS THE magic number in poker. The game began with five cards, and in the years since the invention of Bluff Poker a lot of head scratching has produced odds tables covering every possible hand in five card stud and five card draw. The entire sweaty, hair-raising, heart-breaking mystique of the game grew around five cards and the odds of 649,763 to 1 against holding the top possible hand, a royal flush. And then some unknown genius, quite possibly a disgruntled loser at the traditional games, mortified the traditionalists by throwing a joker into the deck. In doing so, he put a phrase into the English language—"Ah, that's the joker in the deck"—and blasted hell out of those carefully calculated odds.

Without belaboring the odds—who the heck is going to remember them in the heat of battle anyhow—let's take a couple of examples of what happens when just one wild card is added to a deck. In a standard deck there are only four possible royal flushes. Add the joker and there are twenty-four possible ways to hold a royal flush. And those odds against holding a royal flush drop from 649,763 to 1 all the way down to a mere 220,744 to 1. That means if you're playing five card stud with nothing wild you can play 649,763 hands and chances are—remember that there's no guarantee —that you'll hit a royal flush on one hand. With one joker wild, you should hit a royal flush in 220,744 hands.

Now the odds are even better that, while you're busy counting up to 220,744, someone is going to bluff you out on the 189,555th hand with a busted flush, so let's forget trying to remember those odds.

More easily understandable, I think, are the odds against lower ranking hands. In five card stud with nothing wild the odds against drawing three of a kind are 46 to 1. With a wild joker the odds against holding three of a kind drop to 20 to 1. Thus, it is easy to see that the chances of holding three of a kind with one wild card are more than doubled with the addition of a joker.

I salute the fellow who dreamed up the concept of a wild card and I dedicate this first section of game listings to his memory. May he always hold a joker in the hole.

FIVE CARD STUD WITH THE BUG

Form: Five card stud—one card face down, four cards face up.

Wild Cards: One joker—the Bug—which is wild with aces, straights and flushes.

The Play: Each player antes. The down-card and one up-card are dealt, after which the high card bets. There are betting intervals after each of the remaining three up-cards. When all bets and raises are finished, the last bettor or raiser shows his down-card.

Comments: The addition of the Bug to five card stud makes it possible, but highly improbable, to hold five aces. The main effect of the Bug is to make it more likely to hit a straight or a flush or a combination of aces. Hands are fairly easy to read, not much more difficult than reading a hand of straight five card stud. If the Bug shows, for example, in a hand which cannot possibly reach to a straight or a flush, and in which there are no aces showing, the best hand the player could be holding would be two aces, if he had an ace in the hole.

Variations: Both jokers may be used as Bugs. One or both jokers may be used as wild cards—that is, wild all the way. Two Bugs in the game increase the chances for straights and flushes, and if the jokers are played wild the possible value of the hands is increased even more. However, since only one card is hidden, hands are still easy to read. A good rule of thumb to follow is this: If a joker in the hole would make the opponent's hand a winner over your holdings, think of his hole-card as a joker.

What Should Win:

  Flush: Almost always.

  Straight: Most of the time.

  Three of a kind: Good bet unless you're looking at a straight or a flush.

D E U C E S   W I L D

Form: Five card stud.

Wild Cards: All four deuces.

The Play: Same as any five card stud game.

Comments: With four wild cards in the game the only time a pair of aces will hold up is when all the other players commit suicide. Assume that there is a wild card in the hole somewhere and read the hands accordingly. Five card stud with a wild card is a good way to begin to understand wild cards, since all but one card of the opponents' hands are visible. Again, a good rule is to assume that the wild card which could beat you is there. Most of the time it will be.

Variations: Five card stud may be played with any card designated as wild, but one's about as good as another. One-eyed jacks wild, for example, is almost the same game as having two jokers wild. The minor difference would be in having two less cards in the deck if one-eyed jacks are wild and there are no jokers.

What Should Win:

Four of a kind: Almost always.
Full house: Most of the time.
Flush: Good bet most of the time.
Straight: Good in many hands, but watch it.

HOLD IT AND ROLL IT (★★)

Form: Five card stud with cards dealt face down to be turned over ("rolled") by the player.

Wild Cards: The card which is kept in the hole.

The Play: Two cards are dealt face down after a specified ante. Each player turns one card. The high card bets. Each of the remaining cards is dealt face down and the individual player makes a choice *each time* as to which card he wants to keep in the hole as his wild card. There are betting intervals after each card, as in any five card stud game.

Comments: Making the hole-card wild changes the character of the game completely. The value of hands in Hold It and Roll It runs considerably higher than in a simple game of five card stud with the hole-card wild, because on each card the player gets an opportunity to choose between two cards for his wild card. It is possible to hold four of a kind quite often in Hold It and Roll It, and a hand is seldom won with less than a flush or a straight.

Hold It and Roll It is the first of the games listed which is, in my opinion, a true wild game. Don't let its simplicity fool you. The element of choice is very important, with the first choice being crucial. Choosing which card to roll out of the first two gives the player a chance to see if his card sense, intuition or ESP is working. A good or lucky choice can mean the difference between a flush or a straight and a busted hand.

Variations: One or two jokers may be added, wild all the way. In general, the rule in wild-card games is—if there is a stated wild card, then the jokers are also wild all the way. Jokers almost always show up on top in Hold It and Roll It because, after all, the hole-card is wild already so there would be no percentage in holding a joker in the hole. By rolling the joker, the player is assured of at least two wild cards. So, since no one in his right mind would conceal a joker, playing jokers wild adds nothing to the game save raising the value of the hands. I prefer Hold It and Roll It without jokers.

What Should Win:

> *Four of a kind:* Almost always.
>
> *Full house:* No such animal in this game. (See METHODS OF PLAY)
>
> *Flush:* Most of the time.
>
> *Straight:* A good bet.
>
> *Three of a kind:* Only if nothing else is showing.

Methods Of Play: I usually turn out the higher of my first two cards. Usually, the minimum winning hand is a

straight, so I want to start my possible straight as high
as I can. If I'm to end up with three of a kind or four
of a kind I want my highest cards topside. When the
third card comes face down I make a choice between
building toward a flush or a straight, if possible. If I
have two cards in a suit, and they also reach to a
straight, the choice is easy. If, after three cards, I see that
a straight or a flush is impossible and I have not paired,
thus giving myself two wild cards, I usually fold.

What would be a busted straight or flush becomes,
with the wild card in the hole, an actual straight or flush
if you hold the right hole-card. The secret is to turn the
cards so as to always keep the straight within reach,
letting the more difficult-to-hit flush go by the wayside
if a choice has to be made (on the theory that a straight
in the hand is better than a flush in the cards yet to
come).

In the lucky event of holding two pairs, it is important to hold a member of the *lower* pair in the hole
to give yourself the highest possible four of a kind. Two
deuces and two queens become four queens if a deuce
is held in the hole. With a holding of one pair, don't turn
out the pair, even if they're aces, until the last card. Then,
if your only holding is a high pair, it is best to roll the
pair out, holding a lower card as the wild card, in order
to have a high three of a kind.

One peculiarity of this game is the fact that there is no
such hand as a full house. It's easy to see why when you
think about it. If you're holding a full house in five
cards, one card is in the hole and it is wild, making
either one or two more cards in the full house wild with
it. A natural full house, then, becomes five of a kind.

The one disadvantage to this little game, which I
think is the best five card stud wild game, is the fact
that a straight or a flush is clearly visible after all four

cards are rolled. If the four up-cards will reach to a straight or a flush, it's there, naturally, since the hole-card is wild. However, three cards toward a flush or straight plus a pair, one up and one in the hole, makes for some question and gets a call from a lower straight or flush.

Five of a kind happens now and then in Hold It and Roll It. Straight flushes are seen occasionally, but a good four of a kind is a potent hand. A large pair up against you could mean another four of a kind, but in order to have it, the opponent would have to have either two pairs or a third card to match his exposed pair.

One more comment. I suppose, after thinking it over, that a full house would be possible, but only through stupid playing or in a frenzied attempt to bluff out an obvious low five of a kind. By turning out two pairs and leaving an odd card in the hole, a player could hold a full house, but since turning out the odd card and hold-ing one member of a pair would result in four of a kind, this would be foolish play. Two pairs up usually means five of a kind, and it's conceivable that a situation would arise where a player rolled out two pairs, thus signaling five of a kind and a second player, sitting on two pairs and an odd card, would roll his two pairs, which would have to be higher than the other set of two pairs, in an effort to bluff. However, as I've said many times, you don't hardly run anyone with a low-limit bet, not when he's sitting on five of a kind.

SIX CARD STUD

Form: Five card stud plus an extra down-card at the end.
Wild Cards: Any combination of wild cards can be played.
The Play: Deal one down, one up, bet. Bet on each card as it

is dealt. Sixth card is dealt down and after a final round of betting, the cards are shown, with the last bettor or raiser showing first. Five cards are used in the poker hand.

Comments: Playing with six cards adds one more betting interval, but serves little purpose otherwise. Six card stud in various forms is often played when there are eight or nine players in a game. However, with eight players, there are usually enough cards to go around for a full seven card game, if the betting is spirited; someone will be forced out early enough to assure sufficient cards to deal seven cards around.

Variations: All wild-card variations which are possible with seven card stud may be played with six cards. In very large games, eight or nine players, six card stud can be useful with some of the wild variations listed in the seven card stud section.

What Should Win: Add about two cat's hairs to the value of the winning hands in five card games of similar structure and subtract one cat's hair from the value of hands which would win in seven card games.

PISTOL

Form: Five card stud.

Wild Cards: The joker or jokers, the Bug or Bugs, or any other wild card.

The Play: Same as five card stud except that there is a betting interval after the first down-card is dealt.

Comments: Ho hum.

MEXICAN STUD

Form: Five card stud.

Wild Cards: Any card or combination as chosen by dealer.

The Play: Mexican Stud is Hold It and Roll It without a wild hole-card. Each card comes down, and the player rolls his choice until four cards are up, betting on each card beginning with the second card.

Comments: Only slightly more interesting than bare five card.

What Should Win: Same hands as in five card stud. You don't change the spots on the cards merely by dealing them face down and rolling them.

THROW AWAY STUD

Form: Five card stud with a sixth card up or down to replace either the hole-card or one of the up-cards.

Wild Cards: Dealer's choice.

The Play: Same as five card stud, except that a sixth card may be taken to replace one of the original five. If the hole-card is to be replaced, the sixth card is dealt down. If an up-card is to be replaced, the sixth card comes up. It is not mandatory to take the sixth card. There is an additional round of betting after the sixth card.

Comments: Not enough difference to make for excitement.

What Should Win: Basically, hands run much the same as in five card stud with a slight increment in possibilities because of the sixth card.

CHAPTER IV

Wild Games
Based on Draw Poker

WITHOUT LISTING each as a separate
game, I will mention such hackneyed possibilities as draw
poker with deuces or any other card in the deck wild, draw
with the joker or jokers, draw with the Bug or Bugs.

For some reason, there seem to be fewer wild games as-
sociated with the draw poker form. One of the games which
I list, and rate highly—Jacks To Open, Tripps To Win—is
not even a wild game, but simply a variation of draw poker.

SHOTGUN

Form: Sort of mixed up—essentially draw poker with added
betting intervals.

Wild Cards: Usually none, but can be played with the Bug or
any number of wild cards.

The Play: Deal three cards down, look at them, and bet. The
player to the dealer's left is under the gun. Deal cards
four and five down, players looking at them, and bet on
each one. With five cards in hand the game then reverts

to standard draw poker, with a draw of up to three cards and a final bet after the draw.

Comments: Shotgun is listed by Jacoby and others. It's quite unexciting, with its chief value being more betting intervals. In my experience, Shotgun doesn't build a good pot, because sensible players drop out early.

The origins of this game, like the origins of most wild-card games, are unknown. The reason for the name is obscure, but someone once suggested that it's called Shotgun because most players would have to have a gun held on them before they would play it.

Variations: Adding one or two jokers wild couldn't hurt it.

What Should Win: Same hands as in draw poker.

SPIT IN THE OCEAN

Form: Draw poker with a common wild card.

Wild Cards: The card in the middle of the table is wild for everyone—it and all like it.

The Play: There is a betting interval after each player is dealt four cards down and one card is dealt face up in the middle of the table. Then each player is allowed to draw up to three cards. After another round of betting, there is a showdown, with the last bettor or raiser showing first.

Comments: Spit is one of the older wild-card games and is often referred to contemptuously by old-line poker players as being the epitome of evil. There are four wild cards in the game, one of which, the card in the middle, is in everyone's hand. Nevertheless, it's rather tame as wild-card games go these days and is useful only for variety. It does not build much of a pot, since there are only two betting intervals.

Spit got its name, according to one tale, when it was

introduced into a mining camp in the California diggings
during the Great Gold Rush. After trying the game, one
bearded gentleman rose, threw his cards into the camp-
fire and said "I'd as soon spit in the ocean" . . . .

THIRTY-THREE

Form: Draw poker—each player is dealt five cards down.

Wild Cards: All treys.

The Play: Deal five cards down to each player. Treys are wild
and it requires three of a kind to open the betting. If no
one holds three of a kind, ante again and deal another
hand. When a player opens, each player draws up to
three cards and there is a round of betting.

Comments: Not much as wild games go.

Variations: Any card may be designated as wild, but it still
requires three of a kind to open.

What Should Win:

Four of a kind: Rare, but almost always good.

Full house: Most of the time.

Flush: Some of the time.

DR. PEPPER DRAW

Form: Draw poker.

Wild Cards: Tens, twos and fours, and sometimes jokers.

The Play: Each player is dealt five cards down. There is a
betting interval opened by the first player who has a pair
of jacks or better. (With twelve or fourteen wild cards,
that's usually the player under the gun to the dealer's
left.) Each player may draw up to three cards and
there's another betting interval and then a showdown,
with the last raiser or bettor showing first.

Comments: Dr. Pepper is usually played in seven card stud form, but it's not a really bad game as draw. It's easy on the pocketbook, since it has only one ante and two rounds of bettings.

What Should Win:

Royal flush: Most of the time.

Straight flush: Good bet.

Four of a kind: Sometimes.

Full house: Rarely.

JACKS AND BACK

Form: Draw poker.

Wild Cards: None.

The Play: Each player is dealt five cards down. Beginning with the player on the dealer's left, each player is given a chance to open the betting. A pair of jacks or a better holding is required to open. If there is an opener, the hand is played out as regular draw poker, with each player allowed to draw as many as three cards before the final round of betting. If there is no opener, the hand goes "back" to low-ball draw poker (that is, poker with the low hand winning). Beginning with the player on the dealer's left, each player is given an opportunity to bet, with no opening requirements. Then there is a draw and a final round of betting. The perfect low hand is: ace, deuce, trey, four, six (not in the same suit).

Comments: Since there is only an ante and two rounds of betting, Jacks and Back does not build a large pot.

What Should Win: If play is opened by a player with a pair of jacks or better, the hands are, of course, the same as in regular draw poker. Low-ball hands are highly erratic, but a hand with anything from a six to an eight high is a good bet. A low-ball hand with a nine, ten or higher as the highest card is not worth much.

WHISKEY

Form: Modified draw—five cards down to everybody; five more down in the middle of the table.

Wild Cards: None.

The Play: Each player is dealt five cards face down one at a time around the table, with an additional hand being dealt face down in the center. There is a round of betting after the deal. The player to the dealer's left has the choice of trading his entire hand for the entire hand in the middle. If he does not choose to trade, the choice goes around the table until a player trades hands. When a player trades for the hand in the middle, he puts his own hand in the middle, face up, and subsequent players, starting to the left of the trader may trade their cards for all or a portion of the hand in the middle. If the choice goes around the table without anyone's taking the hand in the middle, the dealer either takes it or turns it face up so that the trading of cards can proceed. The game ends when a player thinks he has a winning hand and knocks on the table to announce that he will trade no more. A player may not exchange cards and knock on the same turn. After a knock, each player has one more chance to exchange cards, then there is a show-down after a final round of betting. Any player may knock before the hand in the center of the table is exposed. If a player knocks before this hand is exposed, any player may, on the last round of trading after the knock, take up the hand in the middle.

Comments: Complicated and somewhat blah. A variety of this game, with fewer betting rounds, is listed in some editions of Hoyle.

What Should Win:

Flush: Usually.

High straight: Most of the time.

Three of a kind: Sometimes.

Methods Of Play: It's usually safe to knock when you've completed a straight or flush early.

JACKS TO OPEN, TRIPPS TO WIN (★★★)

Form: Draw poker with an added factor: It takes three of a kind or better to win.

Wild Cards: None.

The Play: After an ante, each player is dealt five cards face down. Beginning with the player to the dealer's left, each player is given a chance to open. To open, a player must hold a pair of jacks or something better. If no one can open, another ante is made and the cards are dealt again. This is repeated until there is an opener. When the betting is opened, each player may draw up to three cards. Then there is another round of betting. An opener, or any other player, may bet as a bluff without holding three of a kind or better. And if any player does not see that bet he is out of the play and may not draw a new hand. Those who have called the bets continue anteing and dealing until someone draws three of a kind or better.

Comments: As you may judge by the three-star rating of this game, I like it, even if it isn't a wild-card game. It is not unusual for six or more hands to be dealt before there is a winner and, therefore, a sizable pot is built. Although it is always difficult to run a player with a bluff in low-limit poker, there seem to be more possibilities for the successful bluff in Tripps than in most other games. And, if one or more players are bluffed out, the smaller number of players in the game makes it even more difficult to have a winner, thus building the pot even more.

Variations: Tripps may be played with one or both jokers used as the Bug. This, however, makes it easier to draw a winning hand and defeats the purpose of the game, extending the play to build a sizable pot.

What Should Win: An opener who hits his opening pair, which must be jacks, queens, kings or aces, has a very good shot at the pot and should bet the limit. If the opener checks after the draw, any three of a kind, however small, should bet.

However, after several rounds in which there has been no winner and sometimes not even an opener, hands tend to get bigger. Four of a kind is rare, but I've seen four kings and four tens in the past few months, plus one small straight flush. The more hands that are dealt without a winner, the more likely it is that someone will hit something higher than a mere three of a kind. Full houses happen occasionally. Straights and flushes are fairly common.

In general, however, short of pat hands and multiple raises, three high face cards warrant staying.

And remember, if you're bluffed out by a bettor, you lose any chance of trying for the pot on the next deal if there isn't a winner.

Methods Of Play: When a player opens he must have, as a minimum, a pair of jacks. If the opener draws three cards, he is drawing to a pair. It is not wise to hold a kicker—an odd card that you hope to pair—as it sometimes is in regular draw poker, since it takes three of a kind minimum to win and a pair or two pairs with an ace kicking is just another loser.

In general, the good draw poker player can hold his own in Tripps. Basically, I always try to draw to a pair, no matter how small, if the opener draws three cards. This draw indicates that he holds only a pair and, even if his pair is larger than mine, if I hit my pair and he doesn't hit his, I beat him.

If the opener draws two cards, I will sometimes throw away a low pair and draw as many as three cards to a flush, since chances are the opener is already holding three of a kind which could very well be larger than my small three of a kind if I hit.

If the opener draws only one card, he is most likely drawing to two pairs and the odds against him hitting a full house are high. In that case, I will draw to a low pair. A pat hand on the part of the opener usually indicates a straight or a flush and necessitates my drawing to a flush, even if I have to draw three cards. If I hold two pairs against a pat hand, I will draw one, hoping for the miracle of hitting a full house.

If, after the draw, the opener bets, he could be bluffing and I will usually call. However, if there are one or more raises and I'm not holding a high three of a kind, a straight or better, I will fold.

If I'm in a position of opening, I will discard one of two pairs, stating that I'm splitting openers if the remaining pair is not jacks or better. The discarded pair is put aside to prove openers after the showdown. If I open on a pair and am raised, I've been known to split my opening pair and draw one card to a flush.

Any player hates to be bluffed out. So most players will call anything short of a pat hand or one or more raises after an opener. Occasionally, some wise guy will raise an opener's bet after the draw on the odd chance that the opener is bluffing, and after several people fold there will be only two or three players in the game to play for the pot. And with two or three players the deal can go around a half dozen times before someone hits three of a kind or better. Meanwhile, the players who have been bluffed out have nothing to do but watch the action.

TEXAS TECH

Form: A mixture of draw and showdown.

Wild Cards: Usually none, but can be played with any combination of wild cards.

The Play: Deal three cards down, bet. Players may look. Deal four and five down, betting on each one. Draw up to three cards, bet. Then turn cards one at a time, betting on each card, until there is one more card to turn, then showdown.

Comments: This game is often called Double Barreled Shotgun, for obvious reasons. Again, it's a mixture of draw poker and stud with more betting intervals than in either of the more simple games.

It's said that Aggies from Texas A. & M. named this game Texas Tech. The Aggies are often the butt of jokes, and they turned this one around. They say that the students of Texas Tech like the game because they can't shuffle the cards too well and one hand lasts all night.

What Should Win: In spite of all the action, without wild cards, the hands are the same as in five card draw.

CHAPTER V

Wild Games

Based on Seven Card Stud

S O M E O F the more interesting wild-card games are based on the seven card stud form with minor or major variations. Such games tend to build a large pot, since there are more rounds of betting and since, with more wild cards in the game, the possibilities of turning a medium holding into something good extend up to the last two or three cards.

Seven card stud may be played, of course, with jokers or Bugs or deuces or any other designated wild cards such as one-eyed jacks, etc.

CHICAGO (★★)

Form: Seven card stud—two cards down, four up, one down.
High spade in the hole splits the pot.
Wild Cards: Deuces.

The Play: After an ante, each player is dealt two cards down and one card up. The high card bets. The succeeding cards are dealt, and there are rounds of betting after each card until all cards have been dealt.

Comments: Chicago is a good introduction to wild-card games which feature a pot splitter. The ace of spades in the hole, either on one of the first two cards or on the last card, which comes down, assures the player of half of the pot.

Variations: Since Chicago is a game with a definite name and a definite form, changing the splitter or the wild cards makes it not Chicago but some other game. However, the joker or jokers may be added. If jokers are used, they become deuces, in accordance with the general rule: when there is a wild card in the game, the jokers are also wild all the way.

What Should Win:

Ace of spades in the hole: A cinch for half the pot.

King of spades in the hole: A gamble, but watch out for raisers. The ace is always good for a raise and spirited raising from more than one player, or from a player with nothing showing on the board, usually indicates the ace.

Four of a kind: Usually.

Full house: Good bet most of the time.

Lesser hands: Only in dull play with nothing showing.

Methods Of Play: Four to six wild cards in a game make for high powered hands. In general, without a wild card in the first three cards and without a high spade in the hole, chances are slim. With five to seven players in the game, someone is going to have at least one wild card in the hole. I think that one of the secrets of playing any wild-card game is to assume the worst in any possible situation, but you will lose money in wild-card poker if you try to play cinches or better—that is, if you stay only with what would definitely be a winning hand. The power of the hands around the table can usually be determined by the number of raises. In a game like Chicago, two people raising usually indicates a high spade in the hole and a potent hand. However, the old warnings against betting on "come cards" that you don't yet have can be modified in a game with four to six wild cards. If, for example, you're sitting on four cards toward a straight flush, the chances of your hitting that straight flush are greatly increased by the presence of wild cards in the game. In poker with no wild cards, the odds against drawing an inside card to complete a straight flush are astronomical, but with wild cards your chances are multiplied. Instead of having to hit one specific card out of fifty-two, you have, with deuces wild, five chances, not just one, to hit. Of course, you want to appraise your chances by checking the up-cards in other players' hands. If you needed, for example, a nine of hearts to complete a straight flush and the nine of hearts were showing, along with two deuces, then you would have only two chances, the remaining deuces, to hit. And there is always the chance that the remaining two deuces are hidden in the hole in another hand.

L O W   H O L E - C A R D   W I L D   (★)

Form: Seven card stud.

Wild Cards: The lowest card out of the three cards which are dealt face down.

The Play: Played as seven card stud, with betting intervals after each card starting with the first up-card.

Comments: Each player has at least one wild card, his low hole-card. A deuce in the hole paired by another deuce either up or down gives a player two wild cards. Thus, if a player shows, say, two kings face up, he has a minimum of three kings. However, in figuring who bets —the high hand showing always bets off—the wild hole-card is not taken into account. Two kings face up are merely two kings, for betting purposes, although it is evident that the player holds at least three kings because of his wild card in the hole.

Variations: Joker or jokers may be added as additional wild cards.

What Should Win:

> *Four of a kind:* Most of the time.

> *Full house:* Good bet, unless you're looking at a larger three of a kind showing or two big pairs, of course.

> *Flush:* Just often enough to make you study the situation closely.

LOW HOLE-CARD WILD—CHOICE (★★)

Form: Seven card stud with two variations—the first three cards are dealt face down allowing the player to choose the card he wants to roll up, and the last card can be taken up or down.

Wild Cards: Low card in the hole.

The Play: Deal three cards down. Each player then turns one card and the high card bets. Betting rounds after each subsequent card. On the last card each player may choose to take his card either up or down.

Comments: On the first choice, deciding which of the three initial cards to turn up, it is possible to keep a pair in the hole, thus assuring at least two wild cards. In addition, the choice on the last card allows a player to keep a wild card he likes out of the two cards he is holding down. Thus, if a player holds two tens in the hole he already has two wild cards and may choose to keep them wild by taking his last card up. If he takes the last card down and it's smaller than a ten his tens are no longer wild. The two choices in this game make for more powerful hands. In low hole without a choice, a player could be, for example, sitting on two or more wild cards. If his hole-cards are a six and a ten and he has paired the six in the up-cards, he has two wild cards. However, when the last card comes down and it's, say, a four, then his sixes are no longer wild, and this changes his hand drastically.

What Should Win:

Five of a kind: Not uncommon.

Straight flush: Good bet.

Four of a kind: Often, but check closely on the up-cards of any player who draws his last card face up.

Methods Of Play: If, out of the first three cards, a player draws a pair, he naturally wants to keep that pair in the hole. By taking his last card up, he is assured of at least two wild cards. The exception to this rule would be when, for example, the holding is two eights and an ace. Then, in order to conceal the ace, it might be good to roll one of the eights. The eights are still wild, since the eight is the low hole-card and can be kept wild by taking the last card up.

If I have three unmatched cards on the first three cards I usually will roll a deuce or a trey and keep two higher cards in the hole. I do this because, in order to have more than one wild card, I would have to hit the deuce or the trey with a matching card if one of them were kept in the hole. By rolling the smaller card it then becomes possible to gamble on the last card, unless developments in other hands make it not worthwhile. For example: I'm holding on the first three cards ace, ten, deuce. I roll the deuce. Then, as the cards are dealt, I hit a second ace. When it's time to draw the seventh card, I'm holding ace-ten in the hole, deuce, eight, ace, six on top. By taking the card down I increase my chances to hit two wild cards and, thus, to hold four aces. I can have two wild cards by hitting a ten, a deuce, an eight or a six, a total of sixteen chances out of fifty-two as opposed to only three out of fifty-two had I held the deuce in the hole.

It is possible by watching how the other players take their last cards to make a more accurate estimate of their strengths. A player taking his last card up usually has two wild cards minimum and doesn't want to risk changing them by drawing a lower card. Thus, you can figure that he has either a pair in the hole or has paired his low hole-card on the board. A player taking his last card down is gambling, trying to pair his low hole-card.

RED BALL

Form: Seven card stud with a killer.

Wild Cards: The two black fours.

The Play: Same as seven card stud except that when any player draws a red four face up he is forced to "go home"—to fold his hand regardless of his other holdings.

Comments: Unless a player knows where the red fours are, say he has one in the hole and another has come up to kill one player, he usually bets lightly even with a strong hand, for there is always the possibility of drawing a red ball and being forced to fold. Thus, Red Ball does not usually build a good pot.

Variations: May also be played with the joker or jokers acting as black fours.

What Should Win: (With two wild cards)

Full house: Most of the time.

Flush: Sometimes.

ANACONDA

Form: Seven cards down with twists.

Wild Cards: Usually none, but may be played with any combination of wild cards.

The Play: Each player is dealt seven cards down. The player looks at his cards and passes three cards to the player on his left. After the pass is completed, each player discards two cards, leaving five down-cards. Each player turns one card, there is a round of betting and this is repeated until four cards are face up, leaving one card down.

Comments: O.K. now and then for variety, but not a really exciting game. It builds the same pot that five card stud builds and is, therefore, a rather tame game in spite of the ingenious twists. Since each player may arrange his cards in any order before beginning to expose them, the hands will be concealed better than in five card stud. A pair turned early usually indicates at least three of a kind.

What Should Win: Hands run higher than in five card stud, but I have insufficient data to predict a winner. The few times I've played the game a flush was usually a winner.

LOW-BALL

Form: Seven card stud with the low poker hand winning.

Wild Cards: Dealer's choice.

The Play: Played as seven card stud.

Comments: As dull as seven card stud with the high hand winning.

What Should Win: In some low-ball games the ace is played as high only. However, it seems logical to me, since the ace is either high or low in a straight or a straight flush, for the ace to be counted as either high or low in the low hand. Thus, the perfect low-ball hand is ace, two, trey, four, six in different suits. Any hand higher than eight-high is risky.

THE ONE IN THE MIDDLE

Form: Seven card stud with a dash of Spit in the Ocean.

Wild Cards: One card is dealt face down in the middle of the table. When a pair shows on the board, this card is turned and it is wild for everyone, it and all like it.

The Play: Each player is dealt two cards down and one card up. One card is dealt face down in the center of the table. High card bets and high hand continues to bet after each card until one player holds a pair face up. Then, after the pair bets, the center card is exposed, and there is another round of betting before another card is dealt. In the event that a pair does not show on the table in the four up-cards, the center card is turned after the fourth up-card and there is a round of betting before dealing the last down-card. The one in the middle is used as a fifth card for each player. Other cards of its value are also wild.

Comments: Each player is assured of at least one wild card. An additional round of betting is inserted when the wild card is turned, thus helping to build the pot.

What Should Win:

Four of a kind: Usually.

Lesser hands: Only if nothing is showing.

Methods Of Play: One is almost forced to stay until the wild card is turned, since, if it hits a singleton or a pair in one's hand, a good hand is assured. Since the wild card is turned on the appearance of the first pair, it's usually safe to stay.

BASEBALL (★★★)

Form: Seven card stud. Fours get a secret.

Wild Cards: Treys and nines.

The Play: Deal three cards face down. Each player rolls one card, or more if two or more of the hole-cards are fours. For each four, players pay a nickle and receive a new hole-card—that is, the "secret" comes face down. After each player has rolled a card and secrets have been given for fours, high card bets and the deal continues with players paying a nickle (or some agreed-upon amount) for fours and wild cards. A four *does not* get a secret on the last card, which comes face down. There is, of course, a round of betting after each card is dealt.

Comments: Baseball is one of the older games. As in most good wild games, the wild cards are based on some idea to enable the players to remember the wild cards and to give a bit of reason to the choice of wild cards. In the game of baseball—played on a playing field and not on a card table—there are three bases, nine innings and four balls make a walk. Thus, in the card game, treys and nines are wild and fours are given a free ride or a walk in the form of a "secret," a card dealt face down.

Variations: Jokers may be added as wild cards, making a total of ten wild cards in the game, four threes, four nines and two jokers.

Paying for wild cards and fours is optional, but is useful in low-limit games to help build the pot. There are several variations of paying for meaningful cards. All cards may be paid for at the rate of the ante. In a nickle-limit game all treys, nines and fours would cost a nickle. Or, you can charge a nickle for nines and fours and a dime for threes.

Baseball is often played in a way which is designed to break up small, social poker games by raising the stakes to rather high levels. In this variation, fours and nines pay a nickle, but a three matches the pot. You won't lose the farm playing match-the-pot in a nickle-limit game, but it can cut severely into the cigar or beauty parlor money.

Let's take a for example. In a six player game the ante is a nickle, making a total of thirty cents in the pot on the ante. On the first round of dealing, a trey turns up and that player matches the pot for thirty cents. There is now a total of sixty cents in the pot. The player who matched the pot now has the right to bet the amount he put in, thirty cents. Three people call. There's now $1.80 in the pot and a trey shows on the second round. That trey matches the pot for $1.80 and bets $1.80, and two players call. There is $9.00 in the pot when a third trey falls on the third up-card. Suddenly, there's significant money involved in a friendly nickle-limit game.

Baseball is an exciting enough game with a low limit. A nickle each on treys, nines and fours builds a healthy little pot and keeps more players in to the last. I don't object to playing a nickle on nines and fours and a dime on treys, either, and I'll play match-the-pot if that's the kind of game it is. I'm just pointing out that match-the-

pot can get out of hand in a friendly game where the
stakes are supposed to stay low.

I've played with players who don't play "roll your
own" on the first three cards. Thus, if you hold one or
more fours face down you don't get to cash them in for
secrets. I feel that players who do not let you roll fours
out of the hole are deluded, misanthropic amateurs who
don't really understand the game of Baseball.

One other mild variation: in a match-the-pot game,
the chances of having to match the pot may be cut by
saying only red threes match the pot.

What Should Win:

Five aces: Only sure thing.

Five of a kind: Usually, but it sometimes takes a high
five of a kind.

Royal flush: Often.

Straight flush: Sometimes.

Four of a kind: When hands are running low and wild
cards are spread.

Methods Of Play: When there are eight to ten wild cards in a
game and you don't have one or more of them on the
first three cards, you're in trouble. A good high pair
might be worth staying for one more card. With fours
getting a secret, there is a chance of getting an extra
hole-card, which helps rationalize staying without a wild
card on the first three. However, wild-card games are
designed to lure the unwary into betting on cards they
haven't got.

I almost always fold if I don't have at least one wild
card in four cards. It usually takes at least four of a kind
to win in Baseball, and I must have three toward that
high four of a kind to stay past four cards. In wild-card
poker, generally, money is lost on the last few rounds of

betting where raises are most likely to occur. You can't be hurt too badly by staying for four cards, unless the raises start early. On an extremely bad night, when you're not hitting anything, you can lose four to five dollars just seeing antes and the first two or three bets, so when the cards are running badly I usually fold earlier unless I have definite prospects.

Sometimes I try to force the cards on the theory that playing scared all the time breeds further loss. This works only a small percentage of the time and can make for heavy losses if continued. By forcing the cards, I mean I'll bet and raise on very little just to show the other players that I don't play cinches or better all the time. Running a long bluff will sometimes cause two or three players to fold, thus changing the run of the cards and, sometimes, my luck.

When playing match-the-pot, I'll stay on lower hands because heavy betting runs more players, thus, usually, cutting the value of the winning hand. A good four of a kind or a little straight flush can take a match-the-pot hand, where it might take five of a kind to win in regular baseball, since more players will stay on low bets. A player holding three of a kind with two cards to come will stay, often, if the bet is a nickle or even a nickle with two or three raises. He'll think long and hard, however, before calling a bet of two or more dollars. Match-the-pot games usually come down to a contest between two players with good hands or, at the most, three players.

NIGHT BASEBALL (★)

Form: Baseball played "in the dark."
Wild Cards: Treys and nines.

The Play: As in regular Baseball, fours get a secret. Deal out all seven cards, face down. No one looks at the cards. The player to the dealer's left rolls one card and bets or checks. After the bet the next player rolls cards until he beats the high hand showing. There is a betting round after each player turns. When it is a player's turn he rolls cards until he holds the high hand at the table or until he has turned all his cards. If a player turns all his cards and is not high, the bet goes back to the player with the high hand. Players may drop out of the betting at any time, of course. Usually played with wild cards and fours paying a nickle.

Comments: Night Baseball can be costly, since there can be many more than the usual five betting rounds. The element of chance enters into the game more than in regular Baseball only because there seems to be a temptation on the part of almost every player to stay in the game longer. There's something about having all of one's card in one's possession without knowing what they are which tempts recklessness. About the only time anyone ever drops out is when he turns all his cards without beating the high hand showing. Actually, the game should be played just as you'd play regular Baseball.

What Should Win:

High five of a kind: Almost always.

Royal flush: Often.

Lesser hands: Only when the situation has shook itself down to limit the possibilities of opponents below the five of a kind or royal flush level.

Methods Of Play: As in regular Baseball, if you don't have at least one wild card in the first three, you're in trouble. With six players in the game, one player almost always has at least two wild cards when all the cards are turned. Thus, a pair would give him four of a kind, or three cards toward a straight flush would make his straight flush. The hands run rather high, as they do in regular Baseball, and since there are more betting rounds the game can cost considerably more.

Sometimes a poor hand shows itself quickly. If wild cards begin to show up early and one player has a large three of a kind rather quickly, then a couple of bad hands will fold themselves out by turning all cards without being able to beat the three of a kind.

Whether to fold or stay can be determined on the basis of the strength of the cards which have been turned up and by the number of cards each player has left to turn. A player who has a large three of a kind with only one card left to turn, for example, can do no better than four of a kind. If you're sitting on a wild card and a high card with five cards left you'd have a good chance to beat him.

DR. PEPPER (★)

Form: Seven card stud.

Wild Cards: Tens, twos and fours.

The Play: Deal two cards down and one up. High card bets. Wild cards have equal rank with aces and the first ace or wild card to the left of the dealer would bet. Betting rounds after each card, as in seven card stud.

Comments: Twelve wild cards, fourteen if jokers are in acting as wild cards, makes for extremely high hands.

Variations: Sometimes a dealer chooses to let each player roll his own. Then, all three of the first three cards are dealt face down and the player chooses which card he wants to expose. This enlarges the chances of some player having two wild cards in the hole.

What Should Win:

Five aces: Good for at least half the pot, since it's possible for more than one player to have five aces.

Five high cards: Watch out for combinations of aces and wild cards.

Royal flush: Now and then.

Lesser hands: Only in the event of divine intervention.

Methods Of Play: I invariably fold if I don't have at least one wild card on the first three cards. I figure every opponent for at least one wild card and possibly two in the hole and if I can't beat that, I quit. It usually takes five of a kind to win. Because of this, many players drop out early and Dr. Pepper doesn't usually build as big a pot as some of the other wild-card games. It's a case of too much of a good thing.

FOLLOW THE QUEEN (★★★★)

Form: Seven card stud, played with secrets and a pot splitter.

Wild Cards: Queens, jokers and the card that follows a queen or a joker.

The Play: Deal each player three cards face down. Players then roll one or more cards with fours getting an extra card, a secret, face down. Players pay a nickle for wild cards and secrets. Dealer begins with the player at his left and gives each player one card face up. If a queen comes up, the player receiving the queen pays a nickle. The next card, dealt to the next player, is wild, (it and all like it) because it "follows the queen." This wild card costs a nickle as well, and if another card of its value is exposed anywhere on the table, it, too, is wild and costs a nickle. There are betting rounds after each completed circuit of the table, just as in seven card stud.

While queens and jokers stay wild, the card that follows the queen, with jokers acting as queens, can change. Each time a queen comes up, her fall kills the previous wild card which followed a queen and makes a new wild card with the following card.

If the last up-card dealt is a queen or a joker, nothing is wild but queens and jokers, since there is no up-card to follow the queen.

A four on the last card cannot get a secret. On the opening deal, each player rolls all his fours, except, perhaps, in the case of a low splitter he might want to keep a four in the splitting suit in the hole at least temporarily. Fours in the hole may be rolled for secrets at any time up to the last card, but not after the last down-card has been dealt. (See METHODS OF PLAY, below.)

Comments: In my view, Follow the Queen is one of the truly great wild-card games and holds its interest over a long period of time because of the uncertainty of the fluctuating wild cards. With four queens and two jokers acting as queens, it is possible for the extra wild card to change six times, thus changing hands drastically.

The origin of wild games, like the origin of jokes, is a mystery. Follow the Queen, sometimes called simply Queeny, may have originated in the army, for I know of people who played it while based in Puerto Rico. The game was introduced to me by an ex-Air Force man a number of years ago.

Follow the Queen is the only game I know—other than one of my own inventions, which is a variation on Queeny—which has the intriguing feature of wild cards that change during play. It is one of the games which sends die-hard stud and draw players screaming for the exits.

The Splitter: The pot splitter is an integral and important part of Follow the Queen and several other wild games. The call of the splitter is at the discretion of the dealer, but it is usually either a high or low card in a suit. For some reason, players seem to favor either the high or low spade. The usual thing is to have the splitter be the high or low card of a suit *in the hole*. When the splitter is played as the low spade in the hole, for example, each player who stays for all cards has at least four chances to hit the splitter, since his first three cards come down and the last card comes down. It is possible to salvage a loser by hitting the splitter on the last card. In addition, for each four, a player receives a down-card, thus increasing his chances to hit the splitter.

Variations: Follow the Queen is an established game with set rules and allows for only minor variations. The game may be played without the jokers, cutting the number of wild cards by two. It can be played as a one-winner game, without a pot splitter, but this cuts down on interest and makes for smaller pots.

What Should Win: If no queens fall or if the extra wild card is killed by a queen as the last up-card, the hand value is considerably lower, since there are only six wild cards in the game. Making allowances for potent combinations showing, of course, a medium-sized four of a kind or a low straight flush is usually good when only queens and jokers are wild. When queens, jokers and an additional card are wild, making a total of ten wild cards:

Five of a kind: Almost necessary.

Royal flush: Sometimes, if no strong combinations show on the board.

Lesser hands: Only if many players have dropped or absolutely nothing is showing.

Methods Of Play: With the jokers in, there can be either six or ten wild cards, depending on whether or not a queen comes up on the deal and whether or not a queen is the last up-card, thus killing the extra wild card. It's feasible, in a low-limit game, to gamble wildly on Queeny, since there is always a chance of hitting fours and getting the splitter as a down-card. Moreover, a pair or three of a kind in a hand without wild cards could become wild if a queen comes up and the following card hits the pair or the three of a kind. Queeny is one of the most ingenious games I know for keeping people in to the last card.

After seeing my first three cards, I will usually roll a low card, unless I'm holding fours or queens. There is one circumstance, short of having three wild cards or two wild cards and the splitter, in which I will roll a queen as my first up-card. If I'm the dealer, and the player on my immediate left rolls a card which matches a low pair I'm holding, along with a queen, I'll sometimes roll a queen. This makes my low pair wild, because his card, following my queen, is wild. This is a gamble, for I'm betting that another queen won't come up during the deal to change the wild card. However, it also acts as a good bluff, since when I roll a wild card the other players have to assume that I'm forced to roll it by holding either three wild cards or two wild cards and the splitter. Usually, a queen will come up during the deal.

If the splitter is the low spade in the hole and I'm holding the four of spades and no lower spade, I'll keep the four in the hole and watch to see if the deuce and trey fall during the deal. If there is no lucky fall of the deuce and trey to make my four good for half the pot, I will keep it in the hole unless a player with no strong cards showing starts raising, thus saying that he has the deuce or trey, or unless there are two spirited raisers. In time, if I'm convinced by developments that someone is holding the deuce, I'll roll my four of spades after receiving my last up-card and take a secret.

I've always been very lucky at Queeny. I tend to stay in the hope of drawing the cards I need and bet more in this game than in any other. And, I will stay on a low bet with no raises to draw the last card if it seems, by the lack of raises, that no one has drawn the splitter. I've salvaged many a pot by hitting the splitter on the last hand.

THE BLIND QUEENY (★★★★)

Form: Follow the Queen played as showdown, with a splitter.

Wild Cards: Queens, jokers and the card that follows the queen.

The Play: Deal each player seven cards face down. No one is allowed to look at his cards. The player to the dealer's left turns one card, then bets or checks. All wild cards cost a nickle and fours cost a nickle and get a secret. After the first player bets, the next player to the left turns cards until he is high. When a queen comes up it costs a nickle and makes the next card in the next hand around the table wild, at least temporarily. If, after a player turns a queen or a joker acting as a queen, he still has to turn cards to beat an existing hand, his next card is *not* the wild card: the wild card is the first card turned in the next hand around the table. Players continue turning only until they have beaten the highest existing hand. If a player turns all his cards without besting the high hand, the bet goes back to the high hand. There is a round of betting each time a new high hand is established.

It is important to remember that a player continues to turn *only* until he has established his hand as the highest hand on the table.

A player is *not* required to buy a secret. If he would damage his chance to have the low splitter, for example, it would not be to his advantage to take a secret. If he chooses not to take the secret, he does not have to pay a nickle for his four.

I'll clarify these two important rules further in the section pertaining to the splitter and in COMMENTS, below.

Comments: In our little club we sometimes call The Blind Queeny by another name—Argument. The Blind Queeny has caused more disagreements than any other single game because the hands are subject to change so often. When seven players are in, forty-nine cards will be exposed if everyone stays until he's turned all his cards, as often happens. With fours getting a secret, it's possible for four more cards to be dealt, making a total of fifty-three cards exposed. Thus, it's almost sure that the wild cards will change six times during the game, making for all sorts of wild changes in the hands. When the wild card changes, all hands have to be reassessed. A royal flush depending on an extra wild card can suddenly become only a busted flush. Two lowly deuces can gain sudden power if deuces come wild.

Since there is so much hand-reading to be done each time a queen or joker falls and makes a new wild card, a hand of Blind Queeny becomes a protracted thing, and only the size of the pots which can be built make up for its length. A pot of four dollars in a nickle-limit game is about standard for Blind Queeny.

It must be thoroughly understood by each player that a player turns cards *only* until he has established his hand as high. This becomes very important toward the end of the game. If a player with a weak hand has turned a six of spades, for example, as his last card, he stays on the chance that his six will be low and will earn half the pot as the splitter. The battle for the high poker hand has narrowed down to two players, one with all cards turned and four kings showing and one with cards still to turn. The man with cards to turn hits four aces with one card left to go. The game is over. He has turned until he is high and *cannot* turn his last card. The six of spades has held up and gets half the pot as the splitter.

If the man who has the high hand with four aces were allowed to turn it is conceivable that he might turn a lower spade and thus take all of the pot. However, the name of the game is turn until you're high and that's it.

There are times, too, when turning the last card when you're already high could be disastrous. Suppose those four winning aces depended on two wild deuces as the extra wild card determined by a prior fall of a queen or a joker. The count shows that there are two more wild cards out and all the fours have shown, drawing secrets, leaving only one card in the deck. Both the hidden cards, the one in the deck and the unturned card in the hand holding four aces are, therefore, wild cards. Turning the last card would kill all extra wild cards, since there would be no card to follow the queen, and the four aces would become nothing more than a full house, aces over deuces, and could possibly be beaten by some player whose hand was changed from a loser to a winner by the death of the four aces.

In that example, the player with the aces would not want to turn his last card, but you can't have your cake and eat it too, so you can't not turn one time to avoid losing and turn the next time to try to win it all.

So, turn until you're high and stop. Period.

The Splitter: The dealer chooses a splitter. It may be the high or low card in any suit. However, a card is only eligible for consideration as a splitter when it is the *last* card turned by a player. If the splitter is the low spade, almost any spade has a shot at half the pot if it's turned on the last card. Thus, if a player has a weak hand and turns all his cards early and his last card is the four of spades, he usually does not want to pay for and receive a secret for his four, since the four has a very good chance of being low and getting half the pot. It is possible, since almost all the cards in the deck are exposed in a seven hand game of Blind Queeny, to count the spades which have fallen and predict whether a spade which appears early on the last card in a hand will split the pot. If the low spades have fallen up to a six, for example, a six of spades on the last card is money in the bank.

Variations: About the only variations possible in this established game affect the splitter. It may be called to split the pot wherever it appears and not just on the last card. This tends to cut the size of the pot, since many players with unpromising hands will fold if the splitter appears in the first few cards.

A definite card can be called as the splitter. For example, deuce of spades *only* splits the pot. This, too, inhibits play. The deuce may appear early as an up-card. Players with weak hands would then fold. The chances of having *a* spade on the last card are good. The chances of having *one particular* spade are not good. The advantage of calling deuce of spades only on the last card as a splitter is to make it highly likely that there will be only one winner. However, in my experience, winning half the pot on a game where most players stay all the way is more rewarding financially than winning all of the pot where many players fold early.

What Should Win: (With queens, jokers and an extra card wild)

Five of a kind: Necessary most of the time.

Royal flush: Sometimes.

Lesser hands: Now and then.

If a queen turns up in the hand of the last player to turn this kills the extra wild card and changes things. There's always that danger, but it can be assessed by counting the wild cards and determining the possibility. If you're sitting on five aces made up of three naturals and two sevens which are temporarily wild and a queen kills all extra wild cards, you're left with a natural full house. Of course, all other hands depending on sevens change also. This last-minute change is hard to predict and makes for some interesting speculation as play continues. All I can say is that Blind Queeny is a *real* gambling game and is not for the fainthearted. With nothing wild but queens and jokers, a straight flush is a good hand usually.

Methods Of Play: Keep the betting low, if you can, until you've seen enough of your hand to know how things are going. If it doesn't cost a fortune, stay to see that last card, which might be the splitter. If you've turned all your cards and have nothing except, possibly, a natural full house, don't bet the farm on hitting your pair or three of a kind with an extra wild card following the fall of a queen. Stay on any card in the splitter suit until it's beaten.

If you turn all your cards early and have a spade with high or low spade splitting on the last card, you can estimate your chances by counting the spades which are already exposed. If all of your cards are exposed and six players have cards to turn, it's going to cost you a lot of money to stay, but it's worth it, since only six remaining cards—the respective last cards of each of the six others—are eligible for splitting. Each time a player turns all his cards without beating your potential splitter with his last card, the value of your hand is increased.

A card near the absolute splitter, or the splitter itself, will, of course, raise at each opportunity, since half the pot is assured or almost assured.

If I have several cards left to turn and other players have turned several, I'm in a position of power. I have a good chance to hold wild cards if not many have turned up, and I bet and raise.

MACKINTOSH (★)

Form: Modified seven card stud.

Wild Cards: Paired hole-cards, one up, one down. A pair in the hole is not wild unless matched by an up-card.

The Play: Deal two cards down, one up, high card bets. The last card is also dealt up, making two down, five up. To have a wild card, a player must match one or more of his hole-cards. A deuce in the hole, matched by a deuce up, becomes two wild cards. If both hole-cards are matched, the player has a minimum of four wild cards. Rounds of betting after each up-card.

Comments: Most confusing thing about Mackintosh is when a new player gets a pair in the hole and does not match that pair with an up-card. This is not a wild combination. However, a pair in the hole matched by an up-card become three wild cards.

Variations: May be played with joker or jokers wild.

What Should Win:

Five of a kind: And they'd better be big ones.

Lesser hands: Rarely.

Methods Of Play: Someone always matches one hole-card early and begins spirited betting. Unless I'm matched or have three of a kind somewhere on the upside, I fold. I'll fold after the fifth card (the third up-card) if I don't have at least one matched hole-card.

WHORES, FOURS
AND ONE-EYED JACKS (★★)

Form: Seven card stud.

Wild Cards: Queens (Whores), fours and one-eyed jacks.

The Play: Basic seven card stud with ten wild cards. Two down, one up. High card bets. Betting rounds after each subsequent card.

Comments: This is my luck-changing game. If I'm unable to buy a hand with anything short of five aces, and I haven't seen an ace in an hour, I'll call "Whores, Fours and One-Eyed Jacks." This shocks the ladies and distracts their attention and I slip in with three of a kind and take a small pot.

What Should Win: People tend to drop out of unfamiliar games. As a result, a medium-good hand can come through if you watch it right. Every player would do well to have a luck-changing game which is played very seldom for this reason alone. But if everyone stays:

Five of a kind: Not uncommon.

Royal or straight flush: Sometimes.

Methods Of Play: About the same as any multiple wild-card game. If I don't have a wild card out of the first three, I quit.

DIME STORE

Form: Seven card stud.

Wild Cards: Fives and tens.

The Play: Fives which come up pay a nickle. Tens pay a dime. Play as in any seven card stud game with two down, four up, one down.

Comments: About the only thing going for this one is its name. It's like Baseball (without the added interest of getting secrets for fours) in that it has eight wild cards.

What Should Win:

Five of a kind: A little less often than in Baseball.

Royal or straight flush: Usually a good bet.

Lesser hands: As circumstances warrant.

Methods Of Play: Fold if you don't have a wild card out of the first three cards, and save your money.

ONE-EYED JACKS, THE MAN WITH THE AX AND A PAIR OF NATURAL SEVENS TAKES IT ALL (★★)

Form: Seven card stud with a grabber.

Wild Cards: The two one-eyed jacks, the king of diamonds (the Man With the Ax). Total of three.

The Play: The grabber in this game is that "pair of natural sevens takes it all" bit. If a pair of natural sevens shows during the play, the game is over. The deal is standard seven card: two down, four up, one down. Betting rounds after each card starting with the first up-card. At the showdown, a pair of natural sevens beats anything and takes all the pot.

Comments: A good game for variety, but it doesn't age well. Two or three times a night isn't bad, but it would get boring if played to excess.

What Should Win: (If a pair of sevens doesn't show up)

Four of a kind: Rare, but almost always good if no possible straight flush shows.

Full house: Often.

Flush: Sometimes.

Methods Of Play: With only three wild cards, the hands won't run too high. The thing to watch is an exposed seven. Any seven which shows up is potential disaster, since a seven in the hole or a hit with a second seven on subsequent rounds would take all the pot. I watch distribution of sevens and bet a good full house. If I'm sitting on one seven, up or down, I try to bet and raise the limit on the twin chance of bluffing someone out and/or hitting the second seven.

FIFTY-TWO (★★★)

Form: Seven card stud, with changes.

Wild Cards: The Bug.

The Play: Each player is dealt two cards face down. There is a round of betting. Five cards are dealt face up in the center of the table with bets after each card. The betting is progressive. The first player to the dealer's left begins the betting with two cents. After the first up-card in the middle of the table, the second player to the dealer's left bets four. Two cents is added to each bet, making the betting run two, four, six, eight, ten and, on the last card after it is dealt, twelve. Raises must be in the amount of or less than the bet. Thus, on the last card, after the bet of twelve cents, there could be three raises of twelve cents apiece, making the last card cost a total of forty-eight cents. High or low spade in the hole splits the pot.

Comments: This is one of the big ones as far as building a pot goes. As far as the poker hand is concerned it runs a little lower than hands in regular seven card stud, in spite of having two jokers in acting as Bugs with aces, straights and flushes. There is no checking in Fifty-Two. A player either bets or folds.

The Splitter: The splitter is dealer's choice but whether it's high or low spade or some other high or low card it must be in the hole. Since the number of down-cards is limited to two per player, the chances of the exact splitter's being held are slim. Therefore almost any card near to the splitter is worth staying on unless there is spirited raising from some quarter to indicate a possible splitter. If the splitter is the low spade, a spade ten and sometimes even higher will take half the pot. Of course, there's always that hand when the deuce itself will show up in the hole-cards. Usually an exact splitter or something close, say the trey or four when it's low splitter, will begin to raise early, probably on the six cent bet. Then, if a high hand jumps in and starts raising, too, you've had the signal and should fold your spade ten or eight. If you're sitting on the splitter or one so close you're sure you're going to take half the pot, it's sometimes best to hold back on the raises until someone hits a high hand and starts raising for you. Raises will often run players, thereby causing the raiser to lose money. And, when you're holding the splitter, the object is not to run people, but to hold them in to build the pot.

Variations: Usually have to do with wild cards. Jokers can be wild all the way. Jokers can be wild with the second card on the board, among the five up-cards, also wild. Or, jokers can be wild with the low up-card. Both variations which make use of an extra wild card from the board make for higher-running hands.

What Should Win:

Flush, two cards of which are in your hand: Almost always.

Flush, one card in your hand: Watch the high cards from another player with a flush.

Straight: Good bet usually.

Two pair: Quite often, if you hold big end of the pairs in your hand.

One pair: Sometimes.

Methods Of Play: A pair in the hole in Fifty-Two is a secure feeling. Because the hands run so low in Fifty-Two, I tend to overstay. Sometimes a good pair will win and, when only two or three people are left, I've seen a pair of treys take the pot. Since you see everyone's five up-cards—the five in the middle of the table are used to complete each player's hand—you can figure the possibilities of someone's hitting a straight or flush. If three hearts come up on the table, it's not too likely that there'll be a flush. If four hearts come up, there is almost always a flush if several players have stayed. Likewise with possible straights. To hold two cards to complete a straight is a tough go, to hold one is almost inevitable.

Odd falls of cards on the board are, of course, to be watched. If two aces and a joker come up on the board, there will be, almost certainly, four aces or, at the least, an aces-over full house.

In Fifty-Two, with seven players, only nineteen cards out of the deck of fifty-four (jokers are in) go into play. In a game of regular seven card with seven players, if all players should stay to the end, forty-nine cards would be in play. So it's easy to see that the possible hands are limited by the fewer number of cards in Fifty-Two. I stay for at least two cards on nothing, and if I hit a pair or am working on a possible straight or flush I will stay longer.

However, in all progressive betting games the time to limit your loss is on the six cent bet. You can ante a nickle, meet the two and four cent bets, and you've risked only eleven cents. Meet the six cent bet betting on cards to come and the investment jumps to seventeen cents, and moreover, the six cent bet is a good starting point for the low splitter to begin his raises so the six cent bet is likely to cost you twelve cents or more.

If I don't have definite prospects I will not call the six cent bet.

CHAPTER VI

The Blockbusters

THE GAME played most by the Oak Island Poker and Lying Club is a little number from out of the west. It's called Forty-Four and it's a blockbuster. It features progressive betting. In progressive betting games, we depart from the nickle-limit rule to allow the bet to go up to twelve on some games and ten on Forty-Four. Playing a hand of Forty-Four with five betting intervals starting at two cents and building to a dime costs a player thirty cents (not counting the ante) if there are no raises. There usually are. Raises are made in the amount of the bet, or less, so an eight cent bet could bring on three raises of eight cents apiece, making the eight cent interval cost a total of thirty-two cents.

A player who wants to stay and draw to his cards can limit the cost in the event there are two spirited raisers by sticking in a raise of one cent when it is his time to bet. Two players working together against two raisers can, by raising a penny each, limit the big raises to one in a game with a three-raise limit, like ours.

But Forty-Four and the other progressive games, such as

Fifty-Two, in the last chapter, can seem costly if good hands hit early and the splitter is out from the beginning. If all possible raises were made in a four-player game of Forty-Four, the total cost to call all bets would be $1.20. In one of the ten card progressive games, the total cost if all possible raisers spoke up for the total potential would be $1.68.

Admittedly, this goes beyond the area of penny poker, but it is very seldom that a hand is raised to its full potential value. The splitter usually waits for the six cent raise or later to raise, and the cut-off method of betting a one cent raise keeps the total size of the pots down. A good Forty-Four pot will give splitters well over a dollar and, on some hands, two dollars each.

The games listed in this brief section have one thing in common. They utilize more than seven cards to build a poker hand. Most of them feature progressive betting and in all progressive betting situations, a player cannot check when it is his turn to bet. He either meets the bet or folds.

The high ratings I give to the games in this section show my liking for them. Of all of them, my favorite is Forty-Four. It is among the most controllable of the wild games and yet it offers variety. The winning hand in Forty-Four can be predicted with some accuracy; there are fewer wild fluctuations of winning hands from five aces to two kings than in some wild games.

I would be interested to know which came first, Forty-Four or Mr. Jacoby's Cincinnati, which we play as Fifty-Five. The games are similar, with Cincinnati utilizing two more cards and ringing in a real whing-dinger of a wild card in the form of Cincinnati Liz. I rate Forty-Four a bit higher in interest and lastability. Either game is a real test for a wild-card player. When we bring a new member into our little club and, after a couple of nights of falling back on stud or draw when he deals, he calls "Forty-Four, Low Spade Splits, Jokers with

Aces, Straights and Flushes," we know he's become a confirmed wild-game man.

F O R T Y - F O U R (★★★★)

Form: Like a stud game, but modified and expanded; best
five out of eight cards.

Wild Cards: The Bug.

The Play: Each player is dealt four cards face down. The
player to the left of the dealer opens the betting for two
cents. The first of four cards is dealt face up in the
middle of the table. The second player to the dealer's
left bets four cents or goes home. The bet is increased
two cents at a time until the four cards have been dealt
face up in the center of the table. After the last bet of
ten cents, the last bettor or raiser shows his cards. High
or low spade (or any high or low card in a suit) splits
the pot. A player may use any combination of the eight
cards, the four in his hand and the four in the middle, to
make the best poker hand. Five cards, never more, are
used in a poker hand. Thus, the splitter must be a part
of the player's hand. He cannot, for example, have five
aces *and* the deuce of spades to take all the pot. However, if the splitter is high spade and he holds five aces
with the ace of spades a part of his five card poker hand,
then he takes all the pot.

Comments: Forty-Four builds a nice pot, has suspense, gives
an opportunity for bluffing on a limited scale. By playing with a pot splitter, the wealth is kept distributed
more evenly. In short, Forty-Four has all the qualities
of a good social, low-limit wild-card game.

The Splitter: With each player holding four down-cards, the
exact splitter is out more than fifty percent of the time.

If the splitter is low spade and you hold a trey of spades, the thing to do is stay to see if someone starts raising the deuce on the six cent bet. I always fold the trey when I'm caught between two raisers. Now and then I throw in a winner when the two raisers, or one strong raiser, were betting on poker hands and not the deuce, but I'm way ahead of the game, because a lot of money can be lost betting on second best in the splitter department.

Variations: Jokers can be called wild all the way. Forty-Four can be played as a one-winner game, eliminating the high or low pot splitter, but it loses some of its interest then, and it doesn't build a big pot.

What Should Win: (When there is no freak combination on the board)

Straight flush: Almost always.

Four of a kind: Happens rarely, but almost always good.

Full house: Usually.

Flush: Good bet.

Straight: Only in weak situations. Bad bet.

Methods Of Play: I have some definite rules in Forty-Four. I stay on a pair or three cards to a flush on the four down-cards. I will, when things are running nicely, stay on nothing to see the first card, since it costs me only two cents. If I don't hit a pair or three cards to a flush then, I'll fold before the four cent bet. I will pay four cents and sometimes match one raise from an eager splitter to see the second card. After that, I will not bet on *two* come cards. If I have, after the second card, two pairs, three of a kind or four cards to a flush, I will gamble, unless spirited raising shows me that someone has already hit his hand.

One raiser indicates the splitter or, perhaps, a flush,

depending on the distribution of cards on the board. Two raisers almost always indicates a high hand and the splitter. Three raisers fighting it out means, perhaps, a full house and a flush and the splitter.

The time to fold your tent is before the six cent bet. You're not hurt badly before that, but from six to ten with raises is where the money is won and lost.

Odd combinations on the board indicate possible freak hands. Two jokers and an ace or two aces and a joker usually means at least four aces somewhere. Watch out, also, for two cards toward a straight flush plus a joker on the board. That means someone has to have only two cards close to the ones on the board to hit a straight flush.

Since everyone shares the four cards in the center of the table, some freak situations bring out identical hands. Four aces on the board could mean two hands with five aces, for example.

If three of a kind show on the board, beware the fourth one. With each player holding four down-cards, chances of its being out are good.

FORTY-FOUR, SECOND CARD WILD (★★★)

Form: Like Forty-Four.

Wild Cards: Jokers and the second card to turn up in the middle of the table.

The Play: Played the same as Forty-Four with one exception. The second card is wild, it and all like it, for everyone. With jokers in the deck, this makes for six wild cards. The betting is progressive and moves around the table on each bet. A player must bet or fold. High or low card in a suit splits at dealer's choice.

Comments: I have included Forty-Four, Second Card Wild as a separate game instead of as a variation of Forty-Four because having the second card wild changes the character of the game completely. In Forty-Four, a flush can be made to stand up. In Second Card Wild, your five of a kind had better be high ones.

Variations: Third card can be called wild and this tends to keep players in a little longer in order to see the wild card. It also keeps *you* in. May also be played with the low card in the middle wild, which changes the character of the game drastically.

Methods Of Play: I stay to see the wild card. When it falls, if I don't have at least a royal flush, I'll fold. Sometimes I'll fold four nothings before the two cent bet. With four small, unmatched cards, even if I should hit during the fall of the four cards in the middle, I'd have five small ones and could easily be beaten.

I will watch the fall of the first center card and if it pairs me, I'm feeling better, especially if it's a high pair. Then if I'm also paired on the second card, which is wild, I'm sitting on four of a kind with two cards to fall. But if I have only one wild card for, say, three of a kind or worse after the fall of the wild card, then I'm going home.

Playing the splitter in Forty-Four, Second Card Wild is a bit more critical, because there tend to be more raises.

KHRUSHCHEV (★★★★)

Form: An eight card game. Four down, four up to each player.

Wild Cards: Low pair, up, down or in combination of up and down. Two jokers wild all the way.

The Play: Four cards are dealt face down to each player. Player on dealer's left is under the gun and may bet or check. After a round of betting, the first of four up-cards is dealt to each player. The high hand bets. There are rounds of betting after each up-card. Any pair may be wild and it can be in the hole, up, down, or one up and one down. In the event of more than one pair, the lowest pair is wild. Of course, if the low pair is hit and becomes three of a kind, all three cards are wild. High or low card in a suit at dealer's choice splits the pot. The splitter must be in the hole.

Comments: Hands run very high, since almost everyone will have at least two wild cards. Khrushchev is a fine, exciting game. Because the betting is regular and not progressive, it builds smaller pots than Forty-Four or Fifty-Five, but the possibility of high hands usually keeps players in, and sometimes the betting will be spirited with hands like five aces, five kings and five queens fighting it out.

Variations: Not many allowed, unless you stop calling the game Khrushchev. It can be played without the jokers, but the charm of the game is its very wildness and taking out jokers takes away some of the flair. It's a lot easier to hit a high five of a kind with jokers in. A low pair and a joker gives you three wild cards, whereas, without the jokers, you'd have to hit the harder combination of three of a kind as your low pair to have three wild cards.

Methods Of Play: One should really have a good shot at the splitter or a pair or a joker on the first four cards to play. However, opening betting is usually low, so it won't cost too much money to see if you hit a pair on the first up-card. After taking one up-card, if you haven't

paired to have two wild cards, you're in trouble. With
four cards coming up to each player, you can judge the
hands in which a straight flush or a high four of a kind
might have a chance. Pairs on the board indicate posi-
tive wild cards for a player. If, for example, a player
shows a pair of queens, a ten and five up after all four
cards are dealt, his queens are wild showing because
they are the low pair; but if he should have a lower pair
in the hole, that pair is wild. Two queens showing makes
five queens so possible that I wouldn't often bet against
it. Remember that in this game a natural full house becomes five of a kind. Two pairs and a joker make five
of a kind. Three deuces and an ace-king of spades make
a royal flush. The combinations are endless.

Not only are there lots of possibilities for high hands
in Khrushchev, but those possibilities always seem to
happen. Hands seem to run even higher than they
should run in this mad Russian game. In general, if I'm
going to stay for all four up-cards, I want a good shot
at a big five of a kind. I'll sometimes stay on a royal
flush with no pairs on the board and with no one betting
proud.

In playing the splitter, you're faced with the same
odds as in Forty-Four. Each player has four chances,
his four down-cards, to hit the exact splitter. The next-to-
best splitter rarely rides home to victory in Khrushchev.

FIFTY-FIVE (★★★)

Form: Five cards down to each player. Five up one at a time
in the center of the table.

Wild Cards: The Bug.

The Play: Each player is dealt five cards down. Betting is progressive, as in Forty-Four, with the player to the dealer's left opening the betting for two cents. Five more cards are dealt face up in the center of the table, and are used by everyone. Bets run two, four, six, eight, ten and twelve. Three raises possible on each bet. Poker hands are formed by choosing the best five cards on the ten cards in play for each player.

Comments: In our part of the country, Fifty-Five is an off-shoot of Forty-Four. This spontaneous development from four and four to five and five leads me to think that, perhaps, Forty-Four is the older game. However, when doing research for this project, I discovered that Oswald Jacoby lists the game in his *Oswald Jacoby on Poker* as "Cincinnati." Jacoby plays the game without progressive betting. This ten card game with table stakes and unlimited raising allowed could be a real killer, much too rich for the blood of us low-stakes players.

Variations: Fifty-Five as a basic game allows little variation save for a choice on the part of the dealer as to which high or low card will split. However, it can be played with the high and low hands splitting. The perfect low hand would be ace, deuce, trey, four, six not in the same suit.

What Should Win:

Five aces: Always possible—especially when a combination of aces and the joker falls on the board—but infrequent.

Royal flush: Virtually a "lock" when only one ace shows.

Straight flush: Most of the time.

Four aces: Good bet most of the time.

Big full house: Sometimes.

Methods Of Play: In playing the splitter, remember that each player has five cards down, so the odds against taking half the pot with anything other than the exact splitting card make a poor gamble. The only time I play the one next to the splitter or worse is when, early, the splitter shows in the up-cards in the middle of the table, thus making my card good.

Betting come cards in Fifty-Five is risky. With each player working with five cards, hands run considerably higher than in Forty-Four. Because of the higher hands, players fold early when they don't have a really good beginning, such as four cards to a straight flush or a good, solid two pairs. With only the jokers wild, acting as Bugs, five aces is possible, but not too frequent. A royal flush will usually hold up, and a good start toward one in the first five cards warrants a stay. One extra card down and one extra card up doesn't make it *that* easy to hit two come cards when the cards are being dealt in the middle, but the temptation is made much greater to bet on come cards. Conservative play and a careful reading of possibilities based on the cards in the middle are necessary.

FIFTY-FIVE WITH AN EXTRA WILD CARD (★★★★)

Form: Just Fifty-Five.

Wild Cards:

1. Jokers all the way and second card on the board.
2. Jokers all the way and the low card on the board.

The Play: Deal five cards down to each player. The betting is progressive, and is opened by the player at the dealer's

left with a bet of two cents. No checking, as in all progressive betting games. Bets run two, four, six, eight, ten
and twelve cents. Three raises allowed on each bet. High
or low card of a suit, dealer's choice, splits the pot.

Comments: With the low card on the table wild, Jacoby calls
this one "Cincinnati Liz," but, once again, he plays it
with regular betting rounds, not progressive, and a
player can check, with the high hands betting off, after
the betting is opened by the player to the dealer's left but
before a card is exposed in the center. Having an extra
wild card and having the jokers wild all the way makes
it a completely different game, with the value of possible
hands running extremely high. The only sure thing is the
exact splitter, for five aces can be tied. Playing the low
card on the table wild tends to keep players in longer.
Playing the second card on the table wild holds almost
all players for two betting rounds. Either way, the game
is wild and woolly and, knowing that it takes fantastically high hands to win tends to send players with poor
holdings home early. It builds a respectable pot,
especially if there is a player raising the splitter and a
player raising a very good hand.

Variations: High and low poker hands splitting. No wild
cards. I don't particularly like high and low hands splitting in any game, but sometimes that form of splitting
the pot keeps players in longer and adds to the money
in the middle of the table. Without wild cards, the game
loses some of its zing.

What Should Win:

Five high ones: So often that anything less is risky,
especially when combinations of high cards and wild
cards are on the board.

Royal flush: Only sometimes.

Lesser hands: This is one of the games which can have wild fluctuations, and in some situations I've seen a full house and even a flush take the poker hand half of the pot. But that was when there was only one wild one on the board and several players had dropped.

Methods Of Play: 1. Jokers and the second card wild. I'll stay to see the wild card on not too much, hoping to hit a high pair with the first up-card and, perhaps, a lower pair with the wild card. After the wild card shows, I fold on less than four of a kind or a very possible royal flush.

2. Jokers and the low card in the middle wild. This one is rugged! If I'm holding a pair of low cards and a pair of high ones, I'll stay all the way, hoping to hit my low pair. I often lose this way, incidentally. Deuces come up in the middle of the board with sickening regularity when you're holding a trey or a four in your hand as the low card and not often enough when you're holding one or two deuces. Freak combinations come up on the board, such as two aces and two deuces or two wild low cards and a joker. Tie hands are common in this one.

Play the splitter as in regular Fifty-Five. With so many down-cards, unless the exact splitter shows in the center of the table early, the card next to the splitter is a great risk.

When playing low card in the middle wild, you need plenty of money, out-house luck and the gambling instinct.

CHAPTER VII

Odd Games
Without Wild Cards

IT CAN TRULY be said that the following games are not poker. But they're gambling games and some of them have caused a lot of money to change hands. The rated games in this section are good for variety in a dealer's-choice game, and a couple of them can be very exciting and build good pots. Acey-Deucy doesn't have much place in a dealer's-choice situation, since it can be rather protracted, can call for more than one ante, and departs from the usual format of dealer's-choice games. Calling Acey-Deucy is almost as bad as calling blackjack in the middle of a game.

ONE-TWO-THREE (★★)

Form: A draw game with three cards.

The Play: The object is to hit the perfect hand which consists of ace, deuce, trey of any suit. Each player, after an ante, is dealt three cards down. The player on the dealer's right may bet or check. After the betting round, each player draws up to three cards. After a second round of betting, another draw of up to three cards, another round of betting and a final draw of up to three cards. Thus there are four betting rounds and three draws.

Comments: One-Two-Three is a nice little game, but it should not be repeated too often, since the novelty fades rather rapidly.

Variations: None, if the game is to be called One-Two-Three. However, it could be played high, with ace-king-queen as the perfect hand. I don't recommend it.

What Should Win: The perfect hand is very common. And winning the pot on a hand higher than four-high is almost impossible. Ace, three, four is not merely one pip higher than ace, two, four, it's quite a bit more risky.

Methods Of Play: On the first draw, I hold nothing higher than one of the cards of the perfect hand. If one or more players have drawn only one card and I'm far from the perfect hand, I'll sometimes fold after the first draw. If all players took two or three cards, I'll hold a four and an ace or deuce and take one card on the second and third draws trying to hit nothing worse than four-high. If a player stays pat on the third draw, I figure him for the perfect hand and if I can't tie him, I fold. I'll draw to two low cards on the third draw if it doesn't cost me more than a nickle.

N U M B E R S (★★★)

Form: Five cards down to each player, as in many poker games, but played by point count, not poker hands.

The Play: Deal each player five cards and put seven cards in the middle, all cards down. The player to the dealer's left is always under the gun and may bet or check. A card is turned in the middle of the table. Players discard, face up in front of them, all cards of that value. Betting rounds after each card is turned in the center of the table. If there is a repeat in the middle—that is, if one card in the middle is paired by another—a new card is dealt to the middle. When the game is over, there must be seven cards of different rank in the center of the table, regardless of the number of repeats. The pot is split between the holder of the high hand and the low hand determined by counting the face value of the remaining cards held by each player. Aces count one or fifteen; face cards count ten, and others count their face value. It is possible to win both sides of the pot by declaring for both high and low, but the player going high and low *must* win both sides or lose all. Declaration for high or low is made after the last card is turned as the betting round goes on. If a player "goes out" by laying down all his cards, he wins all the pot.

Comments: Numbers is truly a game of chance. However there is an element of skill involved in deciding when to drop out if it becomes impossible for your hand to be either high or low. Since there are betting rounds on repeats, as well as on the total of seven cards of different rank, the pot can be built rather high.

Variations: In friendly, low-limit games, the round of betting after the repeats in the center is eliminated.

What Should Win: No set totals can be determined, since the total of the final hands depends on the cards which have fallen in the middle. High hands, however, unless freak circumstances have depleted all the high-value cards, range from the low thirties to the fifties. Aces are to be watched. Two aces in a high hand add to thirty by themselves. The low hand is usually in the range from one to about sixteen.

Methods Of Play: The ultimate goal is to lay down all cards and take the whole pot. This happens, I'd guess, about one time out of fifty. Any time a player gets down to one or two cards, there is a danger of his going out. On marginal hands, I fold when faced with this possibility. Another method of taking all the pot is to declare for both high and low. The only way I can think of to take both sides without going out is to hold a combination of aces, which can count both one and fifteen, and a low card, such as a deuce or trey. Three aces and a trey would count forty-eight and would usually be good. Three aces and a trey would count six for low and would be risky if one or more players were down to two cards or less. If you sit on three aces and a trey and two players hold two cards, with deuces, fours, fives and sixes showing on the board, then you know that your six has a good chance of being beaten by a combination of ace-three, for a total of four for low.

Needless to say, it's very rare that a player wins all of the pot when declaring for both high and low. It's on the order of holding four aces in the original deal at draw poker.

It's hard to tell, short of watching at least four cards fall and matching all bets on the way, what sort of hand you're going to have. Three high cards of a kind give you a tremendous advantage toward the high hand, since the odds against the fourth card of a kind coming up in the middle are high. High hands usually range from the low thirties, if aces are out in the middle, to the fifties if aces haven't fallen. It's possible to figure the possible highs of other players by watching the fall of the cards in the middle. If you hold two kings and high non-face cards and aces, queens, jacks and tens have fallen, you can estimate the highest total of opposing hands.

It's a great temptation to start betting big when you hold four face cards, with, perhaps, two of them as a pair. However, if you're depending on a pair of face cards for a high total, the fall of a single card on the center can take a total of twenty points out of your hand.

Down toward the end, after the fall of four cards in the middle, you can check the cards held by each player and make your decision. If you're in the middle, holding about three cards neither high nor low, that's a good time to say good-bye.

Figure the crude percentages. If three face cards have fallen on the board in the first four cards and you're holding two or more with a value of ten or higher, chances are another face card won't come up. The same with low cards when you're going for low.

Raises and bets can be governed, in the last stages, by adding the possible value of the opponents' cards, based on what cards have shown in the middle and have been discarded.

It's not uncommon for more than one player to be left with only one card at the end. If aces have fallen and you're sitting on a deuce, you have no worse than a portion of the low side of the pot and should raise as many times as possible. But low is a gamble when you're holding more than, say, four, against players with two cards or less.

ACEY-DEUCY

Form: Two cards down. Bet that a card dealt to you face up will be in between your high and low cards.

The Play: Each player antes a specified amount, say a quarter in a seven man game. Each player receives two cards face down. Beginning with the player on the dealer's left, each player is given an opportunity to bet up to the amount in the pot that a third card dealt face up to him will fall between his high and low cards. The best betting combination, of course, is an ace and a deuce. Then only six cards in the deck can beat you, for if you're dealt an ace or a deuce, that isn't between your high and low card and you lose. Play is continued, with each player betting in turn, until the pot is depleted by winnings. In a dealer's choice game, it may be specified that another ante will be made if a player wins all of the pot before each player has had a chance to bet. In the event of a second ante, play continues in a dealer's-choice game until all the pot is won after each player has his chance to bet. After each player takes his card and bets, his cards are placed, face up, at the bottom of the deck. If a round is completed before the pot is won, a new deal of two cards to each player is made without shuffling. When the deck is expended a player does not have to take the last card in the deck, but he may, at his choice. If the deck is used up before the pot is won and there are still players left to bet, the deck is shuffled without taking up the existing down-cards on the table.

Comments: Usually played as a game within itself, rather than as a part of dealer's choice. Some dealer's-choice games rule out prolonged games such as Acey-Deucy and blackjack.

Methods Of Play: Strictly a percentage game. If a player holds a very high card and a very low card, he will most likely bet the farm. The smaller the interval between the two cards, the lower the bet. Acey-Deucy is a killer, since betting the pot is always a temptation and since ties kill the hand—it's always possible to draw an ace or a deuce when betting the most favored combination, an ace-deuce.

SIX-TWENTY-SIX (★★★★)

Form: One card down to each player. High and low with winners being the hand nearest six and the hand nearest twenty-six in face value count.

The Play: Each player is dealt one card face down. There is a round of betting, with the player to the dealer's left always under the gun. Each player is given a chance to take a card up. After this choice is passed around the table, there is another round of betting. The opportunity to take one card at a time passing around the table is alternated with betting rounds until the time comes when no player takes a card. Then there is a showdown: aces count one or eleven; face cards count ten; and others count their face value. It is possible to take both sides of the pot with two aces and a four. Counting aces as one, two aces and a four add to six. Counting aces as eleven, two aces and a four add to twenty-six. If a player elects to try for both high and low with less than the perfect hand, he must win both sides or lose all. Thus, two aces and a trey, adding to five and twenty-five, would be a great risk, since a tie on either end of the count results in losing everything, if a player has declared both high and low.

Comments: If a player is hitting, he may skip a round, as long as cards are being taken, and take his card next time around. This would be done if a player needed, for example, a face card for a value of ten to make twenty-six and the last three cards before his turn were all ten values. He might want to wait, on the theory that four ten spots in a row would be unlikely. However, the game is ended if the choice goes around the table without any player taking a card.

Since you don't bust by overshooting twenty-six in this game—as you do, for example, by overshooting twenty-one in blackjack—it offers fine opportunities for bluffing. A player holding a five or a seven, one point away from a perfect hand, can run his bluff and, perhaps, run other players off a five or a seven.

On the showdown, a five and a seven tie, being one point away, as do twenty-five and twenty-seven. It's common for more than one player to hold the perfect low or high hand. There comes a time when it is of no advantage to raise if it's evident that your perfect high or low will be tied by one or more players. For example, if you have a six and all your raises have not driven two other players to draw more cards and there are only four people left in the game, it actually costs you money every time you bet, since your half of the pot will be most likely split two or three ways. If there's a three-way tie for low in a four handed game, each time twenty cents goes into the pot, the high splitter gets ten cents of it and the other ten cents will be split three ways, returning you three and one third cents for each nickle you put in. An obvious two-way split with four plays left—that is, with one man almost surely tied with you—is merely a break even situation.

Variations:

Four-Twenty-Four: Perfect hand, two aces and a deuce.

Seven-Twenty-Seven: Perfect hand, two aces and a five.
Eight-Twenty-Eight: Perfect hand, two aces and a six.
Etc.

One more variation: Face cards played to count one half.
Playing face cards as one half point usually makes for
more betting rounds, but seems to confuse the living day-
lights out of people. I don't like it. It's also possible to
play Six-Twenty-Six with the high hand betting. However, this delays the game, since it's necessary for the
dealer to count every total each time before calling out
who is to bet.

What Should Win: In a six or seven man game, almost always,
it takes a perfect six or twenty-six to win half the pot.
There are exceptions, of course. When many players go
far over twenty-six and fold, it might pay to stay on less
or more than twenty-six, depending on the exposed point
count of the opponent. And, of course, if a good bluff
runs everyone off low and leaves you the only one, any
card you have in the hole will win. In situations where
you're obviously low, that is, when you're the only one
going low, it's possible to bleed a bit more money out of
the other players by taking one or more cards to your
six after everyone else has stopped taking cards, thus
forcing more rounds of betting.

Methods Of Play: I'll try a bluff and begin betting the limit
when holding a four, five, seven or eight. If one or more
players stand firm on one card after a couple of rounds
of betting and raising, I'll give up and either fold or try
to hit twenty-six. Since all the cards other than the first
card come up, you can count the total of points showing in the opponents' hands and estimate the possibilities.
A ten and a six showing, backed by solid bets and raises,
means an almost sure twenty-six, since there are a total

of sixteen cards in the deck valued at ten. One must remember that a four up and a deuce in the hole is every
bit as good as a natural six in the hole.

It's bad business to stay, taking card after card and
matching bets and raises, when it's evident that one or
more players are at or near twenty-six. You're throwing
a lot of money into the betting in an effort to do no
more than win a share of the pot, not even half.

T W E L V E - A N D - A - H A L F -
T H I R T Y - T W O - A N D - A - H A L F

Form: Same as Six-Twenty-Six, except that face cards count
one half.

The Play: Same as Six-Twenty-Six. Betting round after the
down-card with the player to the dealer's left under the
gun. Cards may be taken face up one at a time going
around the table, each round of choice followed by a
round of betting.

Comments: Although this game builds a bigger pot, because
there are usually more cards involved in reaching the
higher totals, the difficulty in counting slows the game
very much. You'll be amazed at how many people have
trouble counting to 32½.

Variations: Only variation I know is allowing the high hand
to bet, and this slows things even more.

Methods Of Play: Generally the same as in Six-Twenty-Six.

RED DOG

Form: Five down to each. Bet that one of the five beats a
card turned face up off the deck by the dealer.

The Play: Each player is dealt five cards. The ante is a specified amount to make up a betting pot. A quarter in a six or seven man game should do it. Beginning with the player on the dealer's left, players bet up to the amount in the pot that they can beat, with a card in the same suit, a card turned face up off the deck by the dealer. As in Acey-Deucy, if a player wins the pot before others have a chance to bet, the pot is renewed by another ante. After each player has had one chance to bet the game ends, in a dealer's choice situation, when the pot is won.

Comments: This is another one of those killer games which is sort of out of place in dealer's choice, but which comes up now and then.

Variations: May be played with four cards per player.

Methods Of Play: Strictly a hunch-percentage sort of thing. If you're sitting on four aces you have a lock on any card, of course, and will bet the pot. If you have high cards in two suits, there's a fifty-fifty chance that the card turned up will be in one of them.

CHAPTER VIII

That Damned Game

A G A M E called Mortgage was introduced into our poker club recently and it's so terrible I think it deserves a special chapter all to itself. This, in a way, is segregating it, because I hate and despise it. Yet, it has a fatal fascination for many players and might well become a favorite game, since it builds a whale of a pot and gives the died-in-the-wool stud player his day of glory. Frankly, if I didn't like the club members so well, I might just reorganize the club and exclude all Mortgage players. However, they stick with me through the Blind Queeny and complain only moderately, so I'll continue to play Mortgage with them and then, for revenge, I'll deal Mortgage-Baseball with threes and nines wild, fours getting secrets, roll your own and pay a nickle for all wild cards and fours. That gets them, because if anything builds a pot higher than playing seven card stud until one player has won two hands, playing Baseball until one player has won two will do it.

Mortgage is very simple and it's very insidious. Eager players can push the pot to eight dollars in a nickle-limit game, and once you win a couple of those you're sorta spoiled for the relatively low pots which are built with the usual wild games.

MORTGAGE (★)

Form: Seven card stud, but the pot isn't taken until one player has won two hands.

Wild Cards: The Bug.

The Play: Straight seven card stud with an ante. There is a winner each time, of course, with the high hand winning, but to take the pot a player must win two hands, not necessarily in a row. After each hand, there is another ante.

Comments: With six or seven players, Mortgage can go for seven or eight hands before there is a winner. On the first hand, betting is usually low. Everyone knows that there is a good chance of having several hands before someone wins two and players want to limit losses, or investments, until they have won one hand. The betting usually picks up after one or two players have won a hand, with the winners trying to bluff players out. In a seven man game, Mortgage almost always goes at least four hands before there is a winner.

For some reason, players tend to bet come cards more in Mortgage. It's all psychological, because it takes as much power to win a hand of Mortgage as it does to win a hand of ordinary stud. When there are winners, other players tend to stay, desperately hoping to keep one of the winners from getting his second win and the pot.

My dislike of Mortgage is based on my already stated dislike for stud poker in low-limit games. When someone calls Mortgage it means not just one hand of seven card stud, but several. My chances of winning are as good as anyone's, in the beginning, of course, but a hand of Mortgage takes fifteen or twenty minutes or more and concentrates the winnings in one spot. A night can be made with one win at Mortgage, but for nonwinners, two or three hands of Mortgage can mean rather heavy losses. The introduction of the game into our club has raised the damages considerably. Now some of our players, instead of dropping four or five dollars on a bad night, lose ten or twelve. Thus, Mortgage has a corrosive effect on a long-standing low-limit game.

At the risk of being repetitious, let me point out that bluffing is impossible, or almost impossible, in regular stud at a nickle limit. In Mortgage, it becomes doubly impossible and, in effect, a hand of Mortgage is several hands of showdown poker.

Variations: All the wild-card variations possible in any poker game are possible in Mortgage. In it's simple form, the wild cards are usually limited to Bugs with aces, straights and flushes or jokers wild all the way, but it can be played with deuces, one-eyed jacks or anything wild. It's also possible to play the Mortgage form with any poker game by making it necessary to win twice before taking the pot. Mortgage-Baseball, for example, can become dreadfully expensive.

What Should Win: (in a game with two Bugs)

Flush: Most of the time, with full houses uncommon, but not rare.

Straight: Good bet.

Three of a kind: Sometimes.

Two pairs: Rarely.

Methods Of Play: My attack in Mortgage is to try to keep it as inexpensive as possible until I've won a hand and then to bet like crazy on the percentage that I'll win another hand quickly by driving people out. (Foolish, I know.) Actually, about the only approach is to play the game as you'd play seven card and hope for the best.

CHAPTER IX

Four New
Wild-Card Games

I B E L I E V E you may have gotten the idea that I like wild-card poker and that I like variety in games. I do. I like some games better than others and some are so near their point of origin, such as five card stud with Bugs, that I usually leave them alone if offered a choice. After several years of concentrated wild-card play even the finest games become a bit old, and wild-card players are always searching for new games. *Life* magazine, according to research sources, ran an article a few years ago on a new wild game, thus confirming my statement that wild-card players are always interested in new games.

The interest of youthful players in wild-card games also helps to reinforce my opinion that traditional poker lacks interest unless there is significant money at stake. I'm not all that youthful, except in spirit, and think that neither the country nor poker should be turned over to teeny-boppers and unshaven, misguided youngsters, but I find myself in agreement with college age players who think stud and draw are unbearably stodgy.

The literature regarding poker is almost totally concerned with stud and draw and the psychology of gamblers. However, I did run across one article in *Holiday* which mentioned the boom in poker clubs in Gardena, California. A well-printed, expensively colored brochure from Bow Herbert's Gardena Club and Horseshoe Club informs me that draw poker, played either high or low, is the staple of the Gardena poker houses and, interestingly, that jokers are played as Bugs, wild with aces, straights and flushes. So wild-card poker is invading some of the established professional gambling ranks, if only on a low-stakes, social sort of scale.

Poker as played in the Gardena clubs utilizes some rules with which I do not agree. For example, in low-ball draw, the best hand is ace, deuce, trey, four, five. I question that, because a straight is not low, but as long as I don't play at Gardena, it's all right, I suppose.

I thought it rather revealing that Mr. Herbert's house rules number a total of forty-one. It's easy to see that such a situation would call for iron-clad rules covering everything, since players may very well be strangers and since there is more money involved than in our friendly games of a nickle limit.

All games need rules, but I did not think it necessary here to go into the details of all the ins and outs of poker, since, as I said earlier, a player wanting to start playing wild games usually has played enough stud and draw to know the basic procedures and the more or less universal laws of poker.

But I was talking, not about rules, but about how wild-card poker seems to be becoming more and more popular, and how there is always a demand for new games.

Over a period of years, I've tried to become an inventor of new wild-card games, and have succeeded only moderately. The four games listed in this chapter are, as far as I know, completely original, having been fermented in my not-so-fertile brain after a losing night. There is a variety of worth in the four new games. I'll be the first to admit that two of them are merely variations on existing games, but a couple of them have definite possibilities. Ace in the Hole and 7-Up have received moderately good reactions in test runs on my local victims, and some players now deal 7-Up occasionally.

7 - U P (★★)

Form: Seven card stud with, under proper circumstances, a wild card in the middle.

Wild Cards: Sevens, jokers and the card which follows a seven, dealt up in the middle to signify the wild card. The wild card in the middle is *not* wild for everyone and cannot be used in a hand. It makes the other three cards of its rank wild, thus cutting the number of wild cards possible by one.

The Play: Each player is dealt two down, one up. There is a round of betting. Any time a seven comes up, a card is dealt face up in the middle. The other three cards of its rank are wild, but the card in the middle cannot be used as a part of the hand. Jokers act as sevens, and a card is dealt in the middle after the fall of a joker. High hand bets after each round of dealing until each player has two down, four up, one down. If a joker or seven falls in the last hand in line on the last up-card it kills the extra wild card, since there is no up-card to follow it. All wild cards cost a nickle—sevens, jokers and the extra wild cards as well. High or low card of a selected suit in the hole splits the pot.

Comments: 7-Up is, of course, a variation of Follow the Queen, differing from Queeny in two important aspects.

Fours do not get secrets, and when the extra wild card comes up, since the one in the middle cannot be used, there are only three, rather than four, extra wild cards. This tends to cut the possible value of hands slightly. There are still nine wild cards, if the extra wild card comes up, enough for excitement.

Variations: May be played with fours getting a secret. In this case, the first three cards are dealt face down and each player rolls his own, rolling all fours for an extra card. If fours get a secret, the secret costs a nickle. However, it is not mandatory to take the secret.

What Should Win:

Five of a kind: Happens often.

Royal flush: Good a fair percentage of the time.

Straight flush: Only sometimes.

Lesser hands: In isolated cases.

Methods Of Play: The splitter is played as in any seven card game with a high or low splitter. The exact splitter assures half the pot and should be raised judiciously to cash in as much as possible without driving too many players out early in the game. With nine wild cards possible, starting play without a high pair, three of a kind or a wild card is a risk.

EIGHT-BALL (★)

Form: Seven card stud.

The Play: The winning hand is determined not by the high or low poker hand but by the number of eights, either natural or in added combinations. The deal is as in seven card stud with the first round of betting after each player is dealt two cards down and one up. Betting rounds after

each card. The winning hand is determined by counting
natural eights and two card combinations adding to
eight, with aces counting as one. Thus: ace-seven, deuce-
six, trey-five, four-four all add to eight, making a total
of twenty possible eights in the deck.

Comments: An element of confusion is added by playing
combinations of cards adding to eight. However, sharp
players have no difficulty. In figuring hands, consider
the number of cards involved, seven. If three combinations without a natural eight appear in one hand, that
takes up six cards. The highest possible hand is five
eights, made up of four naturals and one combination or
three naturals and two combinations. In the length of
time we've been playing the game, I haven't seen five
eights. Four eights can be formed by holding four naturals, three naturals and one combination, two naturals
and two combinations or one natural and three combinations. Four eights is an almost sure winner.

Variations: The game may be played as poker with eights and
combinations totaling eight wild. This isn't as wild as it
sounds, although there is a possible total of twenty wild
cards and combinations in the deck. When playing eights
and combinations of eight wild, two cards adding to
eight act as one card *only*. For example, a combination
of ace-seven could not be played both as an eight and as
an ace. Eight-Ball with eights and combinations of eights
wild seems to me to offer some real possibilities, and it
seems to be on the way toward becoming a standard
game in our gatherings.

In either straight Eight-Ball or Eight-Ball with Eights
and Combinations, an additional complicating factor
may be added. Combinations which *subtract* to eight
may also be used. Aces count one or eleven. Ace-trey,
face card-deuce, nine-ace would, thus, add three more

possible combinations to the game. The gain, in my opinion, does not make up for the confusion involved in counting hands.

What Should Win:
Eight-Ball:

Four eights: Practically a lock.

Three eights: Almost always good for at least half the pot.

Two eights: Enough of the time to make it a fair bet unless beaten on the face.

Eight-Ball with Eights and Combinations Adding to Eight Wild:

Straight flush: Almost always.

Four of a kind: Very good bet.

Full house: Hard to hold, because of the number of cards required to form it, but usually good.

Flush: Worth staying on much of the time.

Methods Of Play: Either an eight, a combination or a possible combination is sufficient to risk staying on the first three cards. In straight Eight-Ball, the hands run low. Three eights are usually good for a portion, at least, of the pot and often two eights split. Natural eights are, of course, like money in the bank.

I stay in straight Eight-Ball on two eights or combinations adding to eight.

With eights and combinations of eight wild, it's a new game, and I was tempted to list eights wild as a separate thing altogether. I think, if the game is played a lot, it might eventually shake down to the more complicated form, with eights and combinations of eight wild. Straight Eight-Ball doesn't build spectacular pots. With eights and combinations wild, the pot grows.

Don't let the number of possible combinations fool you into quitting too soon. The number of combinations held in any particular hand is limited by the number of cards. Three combinations, for example, would mean only four of a kind, for the three combinations use six cards, leaving the seventh card to determine the value of the four of a kind. It's possible to hold five of a kind, but unlikely.

I stay with one wild card to see what happens and will stick around with two to the end.

MATINEE

Form: Seven card stud.

Wild Cards: Aces (ones), threes and fives.

The Play: Same as any seven card stud game. Two down, one up, bet. Bet after each card. Last card down.

Comments: Perhaps the weakest of my original games. The only difference between Matinee and Dr. Pepper is that Matinee uses a splitter and Dr. Pepper has tens, twos and fours wild instead of ones, threes and fives. The game is inspired, of course, by the times for matinee performances in movie houses. Its main uses is variety. And, if you've not been hitting the wild cards in other games, Matinee might change your luck, since it uses cards which are not usually played as wild ones.

Variations: Jokers added to make a total of fourteen wild damned cards.

What Should Win:

Five aces: Gets at least half the pot.

Five of a kind: Takes it most of the time.

Lesser hands: Judge the situation by up-cards and be very conservative.

Methods Of Play: With twelve or fourteen wild cards, I must have at least one on the first three cards. By not rolling your own, that is by dealing two down and one up instead of three down and letting a player turn his choice, the chances of the exact splitter being in the hole are lessened. In addition, dealing the third card up exposes more wild cards. If, for example, a player holds only one wild card and it came to him on the third down-card in roll your own, chances are he'd conceal it. By dealing the third card up, the wild card is exposed.

Hands run very high. Unless I'm working on something very definite, like a good five of a kind or a royal flush at a minimum, I forget it. But if I stay for five or six cards, I'll stay, if there are not multiple raises, to try to draw the splitter on the last card.

ACE IN THE HOLE (★★)

Form: Seven card stud.

Wild Cards: Player's choice if he has an ace in the hole.

The Play: Three cards down, roll your own. Bet after third card is turned by all players. Betting rounds as in seven card stud. To hold a wild card, a player must have an ace in the hole either on the first three cards or on the last card, which comes down. He then may choose any card in his hand, it and all like it, as his wild card. He may choose a pair or three or four of a kind as his wild cards.

Comments: How often do aces appear in the hole in seven card stud? That's the odds you're fighting. Of course, an ace in the hole on the first three cards puts you in the catbird's seat. You're going to have at least one wild card. You'll have two wild cards if you hit a pair, three if you hit a natural three of a kind. It's hairy, my friends. And I love it. I'd give the game a higher rating if people weren't scared of it. The few times I've played it, players without an ace in the hole folded out quickly. It isn't necessary to do this, because all sorts of possibilities exist. A player may hold an ace in the hole and not hit a pair. Thus, he has only one wild card and his best hand would be a straight or a flush. A player with an ace in the hole and a pair of wild cards—remember the ace isn't wild, it just allows you to choose a wild card—isn't in the chips necessarily. Two wild cards can end up as nothing better than three aces. I've seen the game taken by a natural flush without wild cards. And there's always the gambling possibility of hitting an ace on that last card, thus letting you choose a wild card from your hand.

If I'm sitting on three of a kind, two pairs, a possible straight flush or a good, high straight, I'll gamble, short of calling multiple raises.

Variations: I think the element of uncertainty is enough without adding jokers as wild cards, but you may, if you like.

What Should Win: I've covered this, too. This game is harder than most to compartmentalize. With aces in the hole, a high five of a kind is necessary sometimes; however, if the aces aren't hit by a pair or a three of a kind to make multiple wild cards, a good flush can win.

One thing I like about this game is the possibilities it offers for bluffing. You can run someone with three of a kind showing on your up-cards by betting and raising like crazy, because he's going to assume that you have your ace in the hole and, thus, multiple wild cards. Give it a try.

In general, about the winning hand, I'd say bet five

high ones like crazy and hang tight on anything less unless other players look weak.

Methods Of Play: I talked about my theory of play in the above COMMENTS. I'll add this. Ace in the Hole can fluctuate wildly and requires alertness. It's possible for no player to have an ace in the hole, and then the game reverts to straight seven card without a wild card. Winning hands can range all the way from five aces down to a good, solid pair, just as in seven card stud. However, there's always the possibility, especially when looking at pairs on the board, that the opponent has that ace and, thus, has a fist full of wildies. Since I invented the game, I tend to be wildly optimistic when I play it, but I'd advise conservatism until you get the hang of it, the feel of it.

Every game has its own feel and the difficult part of learning a new wild game is not learning the rules. They're usually pretty simple. The hard thing is getting the *feel* of what should win. I'll admit that I haven't arrived at any solid conclusions about Ace in the Hole. I watch for aces; an ace up makes the chances of someone's having an ace in the hole just that much less. I watch for pairs on the boards and potent possibilities.

A Final Word

T H E G A M E S in this book have been accumulated over a period of some thirty years in Oklahoma, North Carolina, Tennessee, California and Florida. The majority of them were acquired in a small coastal community just west of the Cape of Fear—where the east coast runs east to west—with a wintertime population of about two hundred people. It is extremely presumptuous of me, with my limited experience, to offer this book as anything more than a compendium of wild-card poker. I'm sure that somewhere there are people playing a wild-card game which would take our little poker club by storm. If one should surface as a result of this book, I'll be grateful.

So this, then, is an invitation to any reader to establish communication via the publisher. If you know a wild-card game not listed here, let's exchange notes about it.

Already, in the writing, I've had one contribution too late to include. Briefly, all red cards are wild, but the wild cards are only good with black aces and black queens. Hummm. My correspondent said it was his favorite wild-card game.

Any other ideas?

Appendix

BEST WILD-CARD GAMES IN BRIEF

THE FOLLOWING is a list of what I consider to be the best of the wild-card games in this book with a very brief statement of how they are played. This section is merely a supplement to the detailed analysis of all games in other sections of the book and is meant to serve as an aid to memory and to be handy for quick reference.

The games are arranged alphabetically beginning with four-star games and dwindling down to those rated with only one star.

FOUR-STAR GAMES

Blind Queeny:
Seven cards down. No one looks at the cards. Play as

showdown with player at dealer's left turning one card to bet or check. Next player turns until he has top hand. Betting round after each high hand is established. Queens and jokers wild, as is the card in the next hand that follows a queen or joker. Fours get secrets. Pay a nickle for all wild cards and secrets. Turn *only* until you're high, then stop. Taking secret and paying for it is optional. High or low splitter on last card turned in each hand.

Follow the Queen:

Seven card stud form with first three cards down. Roll your own with fours paying a nickle for secrets. Queens, jokers and the card that follows a queen or joker wild. Pay a nickle for wild cards. If a queen or joker falls on the last up-card, it kills the extra wild card. High or low splitter in the hole.

Forty-Four:

Best five of eight cards dealt four down to each player, four up in the middle. Bet progressively as four cards are dealt face up in the center of the table. Jokers wild as Bugs. High or low splitter in the hole. No checking. Bet begins after first four cards with player to dealer's left and moves around the table.

Khrushchev:

Best five of eight cards dealt four down at once, then four up one at a time around the table. Betting after the first four, and after each successive card. Low pair, up, down, or in combination, is wild. Jokers wild. High or low splitter in the hole. Regular betting to set limit.

Six-Twenty-Six:

Hands nearest to six and nearest to twenty-six split the pot. Card count is: aces, one or eleven; faces, ten;

others, face value. Player to dealer's left always under the gun. After opening round of betting on first card dealt face down, players take cards one at a time going around the table. Bet after each round of choice cards. Showdown when no one takes a card on a round. No busting—twenty-seven is as good as twenty-four. Tie hands, either high or low, split the half of the pot to which they apply. (Two aces and a four, adding to both six and twenty-six take all of the pot.)

THREE-STAR GAMES

Baseball:

Seven card stud. Last card down. Threes and nines wild. Fours roll and get a secret except on the last card. Pay a nickle for wild cards and secrets.

Baseball With the Jokers:

Same as above, except that jokers are also wild.

Fifty-Five:

Best five of ten cards, five down to each player, five up one at a time in the middle. Betting is progressive, beginning after the five down-cards are dealt moving around the table to the left. No checking. High or low splitter in the hole. The Bug wild.

Fifty-Five With Extra Wild Card:

Same as above, except that the second card on the table or the low card coming up on the table is also wild. Jokers wild all the way. High or low splitter.

Fifty-Two:

Two down to each player, five up in the middle. Progressive betting, beginning after the two down-cards are dealt. High or low splitter in the hole. The Bug.

Numbers:

High and low point count split. Five cards down to each player. Player to dealer's left under the gun. Betting begins after the deal of down-cards. Seven *different* cards, to be matched from player's hands, come face up on the table with betting rounds after each card and after repeats. Count: aces, one or fifteen; faces, ten; others, face value. Ties split that half of the pot to which they pertain.

Seven-Twenty-Seven and other combinations:

Same as Six-Twenty-Six.

TWO-STAR GAMES

Ace in the Hole:

Seven card stud with an ace in the hole, either on the first two cards or the last, allowing a player to choose his own wild card from his hand. The card chosen, it and all like it, act as wild cards in that hand.

Chicago:

Seven card stud with the high spade in the hole splitting the pot. Deuces wild.

Eight-Ball With Eights and Combinations Adding to Eight Wild:

Seven cards, three down, four up, one down. Played as seven card stud with eights and two card combinations adding to eight (e.g., ace-seven, trey-five) acting as wild cards. Two card combinations are played as one card, an eight.

Fifty-Two With Jokers and an Extra Card Wild:

Two down to each player. Five up one at a time in the

center with progressive betting beginning after the down-cards are dealt. Jokers are wild with either the second card coming up on the table or the low card coming on the table also wild. High or low splitter in the hole.

Hold It and Roll It:

Five card stud with *all* cards dealt *down* and the card kept in the hole wild. Deal two, roll one, bet. Bet on each subsequent card. Final hole card and all like it wild.

Jacks To Open, Tripps to Win:

Draw poker requiring a pair of jacks or better to open the betting and three of a kind or better to win. If there is no winner, another ante is made and a new deal comes. Players must call all bets or they're out of the next hand if there is no winner.

Jacks To Open, Tripps To Win With the Bug:

Draw poker. Pair of jacks or better can open betting. Takes three of a kind or better to win. No winner, ante again and deal again. Players meet all bets or may not play in the next hand if there is no winner. Jokers wild as Bugs.

Low Hole-Card—Choice:

Seven card stud with the low card out of the three hole-cards wild, it and all like it. Three down, roll one, bet. Bet on subsequent cards. Player may take last card up or down.

One-Eyed Jacks, The Man With the Ax and a Pair of Natural Sevens Takes It All:

Seven card stud with one-eyed jacks and the king of diamonds wild. Two natural sevens, up, down or in combination, win all. Two pairs of natural sevens in different hands split the pot.

One-Two-Three:

Perfect hand out of three cards is ace-deuce-trey. Each player gets three cards, player to dealer's left bets, each player draws up to three cards. Total of three draws and four rounds of betting.

7-Up:

Seven card stud with sevens, jokers and the card following a seven or joker wild. But wild card comes in the middle and cannot be used in hands, thus it merely makes the other three cards of its rank wild. Pay a nickel on wild cards. High or low splitter in the hole.

Whores, Fours and One-Eyed Jacks:

Seven card stud with queens, fours and the two one-eyed jacks wild.

ONE-STAR GAMES

Dr. Pepper:

Seven card stud with tens, twos and fours wild.

Eight-Ball:

Seven card stud form. Object of game to hold highest number of eights in naturals or two card combinations adding to eight. May also be played with combinations in two cards subtracting to eight. Examples: ace-seven= 8; five-trey=8; etc. Also, if subtracting, face or ten-deuce=8; ace-trey=8.

Fifty-Five High-Low:

Best five of ten cards with high and low poker hands splitting the pot. Perfect low: ace, deuce, trey, four, six, in odd suits. Five down to each player, bet two cents.

Five come up in the middle. Progressive betting. The
Bug wild.

Hold It And Roll It With Jokers Wild:

Five card stud. All cards come down. Jokers and the
card in the hole wild. Bet after dealing two cards down
and turning one. Bet subsequent cards after each is
turned.

Low Hole:

Low hole-card wild in seven card stud.

Mackintosh:

Seven card stud—two down, five up. Bet after first three
and on subsequent cards. Pairing a hole-card makes it
and all like it wild, but must be paired up, not a pair in
the hole.

Mortgage:

Seven card stud with the Bug, played until one player
wins two hands, not necessarily in a row.

Night Baseball:

Seven cards face down. No one looks. Threes, nines and
possibly jokers wild. Fours get a secret. Pay a nickle for
all wild cards and secrets. Played as showdown with
player at dealer's left turning one card to bet or check.
Bet each time a new high hand is established.

Index